At Home with Grief

What would you say to a deceased loved one if they could come back for one day? What if you can't just 'move on' from grief? *At Home with Grief: Continued Bonds with the Deceased* chronicles Blake Paxton's autoethnographic study of his continued relationship with his deceased mother.

In the 1990s, Klass, Silverman, and Nickman argued that after the death of a loved one, the bond does not have to be broken and the bereaved can find many ways to connect with memories of the dead. Building on their work, many other bereavement scholars have discussed the importance of not treating these relationships as pathological and have suggested that more research is needed in this area of grief studies. However, very few studies have addressed the communal and everyday subjective experiences of continuing bonds with the deceased, as well as how our relationship with our grief changes in the long term.

In this book, Blake Paxton shows how a community in southern Illinois continues a relationship with one deceased individual more than ten years after her death. Through this gripping autoethnographic account of his mother's struggles with a rare cancer, her death, and his struggles with his own sexuality, he poses possibilities of what might happen when cultural prescriptions for grief are challenged and how continuing our bonds with our loved ones after their death may help us continue or restore our broken bonds with the living.

Blake Paxton is an assistant professor of communication at Saint Xavier University in Chicago, Illinois, USA. He has published and presented research in the areas of interpersonal and family communication, health and end of life communication, and women's and gender studies. Paxton is a member of several professional organizations, including the International Congress of Qualitative Inquiry, the Organization for the Study of Language, Gender, and Communication, and the National Communication Association.

WRITING LIVES
Ethnographic Narratives
Series Editors: Arthur P. Bochner, Carolyn Ellis and Tony E. Adams
University of South Florida and *Northeastern Illinois University*

Writing Lives: Ethnographic Narratives publishes narrative representations of qualitative research projects. The series editors seek manuscripts that blur the boundaries between humanities and social sciences. We encourage novel and evocative forms of expressing concrete lived experience, including autoethnographic, literary, poetic, artistic, visual, performative, critical, multi-voiced, conversational, and co-constructed representations. We are interested in ethnographic narratives that depict local stories; employ literary modes of scene setting, dialogue, character development, and unfolding action; and include the author's critical reflections on the research and writing process, such as research ethics, alternative modes of inquiry and representation, reflexivity, and evocative storytelling. Proposals and manuscripts should be directed to abochner@usf.edu, cellis@usf.edu or aeadams3@neiu.edu.

Other Volumes in This Series Include:

Young, Gifted and Fat
An Autoethnography of Size, Sexuality, and Privilege
Sharrell D. Luckett

White Folks
Race and Identity in Rural America
Timothy J. Lensmire

Autobiography of a Disease
Patrick Anderson

Searching for an Autoethnographic Ethic
Stephen Andrew

For a full list of titles in this series, please visit www.routledge.com/Writing-Lives-Ethnographic-Narratives/book-series/WLEN.

AT HOME WITH GRIEF
Continued Bonds with the Deceased

Blake Paxton

Routledge
Taylor & Francis Group
NEW YORK AND LONDON

First published 2018
by Routledge
711 Third Avenue, New York, NY 10017

and by Routledge
2 Park Square, Milton Park, Abingdon, Oxon, OX14 4RN

Routledge is an imprint of the Taylor & Francis Group, an informa business

© 2018 Taylor & Francis

The right of Blake Paxton to be identified as author of this work has been asserted by him in accordance with sections 77 and 78 of the Copyright, Designs and Patents Act 1988.

All rights reserved. No part of this book may be reprinted or reproduced or utilised in any form or by any electronic, mechanical, or other means, now known or hereafter invented, including photocopying and recording, or in any information storage or retrieval system, without permission in writing from the publishers.

Trademark notice: Product or corporate names may be trademarks or registered trademarks, and are used only for identification and explanation without intent to infringe.

Library of Congress Cataloging-in-Publication Data
Names: Paxton, Blake, author.
Title: At home with grief : continued bonds with the deceased / Blake Paxton.
Description: New York, NY : Routledge is an imprint of the Taylor & Francis Group, an Informa Business, 2018. | Includes bibliographical references and index.
Identifiers: LCCN 2017041967 | ISBN 9781138747043 (hbk) | ISBN 9781138897618 (pbk) | ISBN 9781315178820 (ebk)
Subjects: LCSH: Grief.
Classification: LCC BF575.G8 P39 2018 | DDC 155.9/37—dc23
LC record available at https://lccn.loc.gov/2017041967

ISBN: 978-1-138-74704-3 (hbk)
ISBN: 978-1-138-89761-8 (pbk)
ISBN: 978-1-315-17882-0 (ebk)

Typeset in ITC Legacy Serif
by Apex CoVantage, LLC

FOR MY FAMILY

FOR MY FAMILY

CONTENTS

Acknowledgments ix

Introduction: The Rendezvous 1
1 Goodbye 9
2 Re-Membering 40
3 Home 65
4 Reassessing Continuing Bonds and Challenging
   the Causality Thesis 110
5 Future Directions for Continuing Bonds Research 131

Afterword: A Family Wedding Reception to Re-Member 145
Appendix: Methodology and Analysis as Mourning 149
References 163
Index 171

ACKNOWLEDGMENTS

Writing this book has been a challenging but satisfying experience. I would like to thank several people for their support in this process.

Thank you Carolyn Ellis, my mother mentor. I have profound gratitude for your guidance over the years. Thank you for helping me find my academic voice and being like family to me.

To fellow editors of the Writing Lives series, Tony Adams and Arthur P. Bochner: your loving support and feedback have been invaluable. I have grown so much as a scholar and writer under your mentorship. I hope this book makes you proud.

Thanks to my father, Lindon Paxton; my stepmother, Kelly Paxton; and my brother, Kyle Paxton, for your encouragement and participation in this project.

To my mother's sisters, Patty Aue, Cindy Heape, Janet McCurdy, and Susie Johnson: You have been the best aunts, supporting me in all of my pursuits. I have enjoyed our numerous conversations and laughing together about Mom. She was lucky to have you in her life—and I will forever admire your sisterhood.

Thank you to my countless family members and friends who contributed to the research process, especially Jill Asbury, Randee Bastien, Kathy Beard, Toni Behm, Kathy Bell, Lisa Coleman, Bitty Craig, Denise and Brett Crain, Linda Davis, Susan Harsha, Susan Heape, Jill and Tim Leake, Karen Malone, Ronna Martin, Jean Ann Mathis, Pam Pursell, Kristy Sanders, Shelley Schantz, Kellie Swayne, and Jim and Kelly

Standley. Your stories of Mom have breathed life into this book and have helped me feel close to her again.

To all of my academic mentors in my undergraduate and graduate studies—Elizabeth Bell, Keith Berry, Ken Cissna, Debra Dobbs, Stacy Holman Jones, Margarethe Kusenbach, Lori Roscoe, and Paaige Turner—your dedication to transformative pedagogy formed me into the scholar that I am today.

To Tasha R. Dunn, my best friend and sister by choice: Through various personal and professional struggles, you have always been there for me. I am so thankful for your friendship, and I wish you all the best in your academic career.

To my numerous esteemed colleagues and friends, from today and the past—Jacob Abraham, Ariane Anderson, Ben Anderson, Jacquelyn Arcy, Ambar Basu, Jennifer Bender, Kristen Blinne, Robin Boylorn, Trevor Clark, Anne Copeland, Summer Renee Cunningham, Heather Curry, Lindy Davidson, Vince Davis, Rachel Dubrofksy, Niki Ellis, Amanda Firestone, Christine Fojtik, Justin Gimotea, Cynthia Grobmeier, Andrew Hermann, Nathan Hodges, Nancie Hudson, Jacob Jenkins, Elizabeth Jeter, Steve Johns, Charles Jones, Jane Jorgenson, Dustin Lemke, Brad Mello, Alisha Menzies, Sarah McGhee, W. Benjamin Myers, Heidi Paintner, Michelle Pepito, Angela Pirlott, David Purnell, Patrick and Stephanie Quarles, Anna and John Richert, Kim Rivard, Cristina Salvador, Renee Robinson, Jessica Ryan, Rachel Severson, Garrett Severson, Rachel Silverman, Joe Smith, Makebba Spears, Lisa Spinazola, Jillian Tullis, Megan Wood-Gillette, Alex Young, and members of the Chicago Gay Men's Chorus—I cherish the moments we have had throughout the years, and I'm forever grateful for your loving community.

To my late grandmother Jo-Ann Strong: I know you loved my mother dearly, and I am happy that the two of you are finally reunited.

Last but certainly not least, I owe all my work to my late mother, Ann Paxton. I hope this serves as a loving testament to the beautiful life you led. You will always be my best friend and hero. I love you.

INTRODUCTION
The Rendezvous

I seek my mother's voice.

Late at night, when my father and stepmother are fast asleep and my younger brother is spending time with friends, I search for her voice. I feel as if I'm part of a pair of star-crossed lovers in a romance novel, and I am prepping for a rendezvous with my mate. Why am I worried about being caught? Why must I do this alone? Am I ashamed of my grief?

I reach under my bed and pull out a box of old VHS tapes that my Aunt Susie gave me three days ago, when I asked to borrow some home videos with Mom in them. "I need them for a research project," I'd said. This was partly true, but I also desired the presence of my mother. Maybe I believe that seeing her move and hearing her speak on these tapes will somehow resurrect her. Somehow resurrect me.

Quickly, I pull on a pair of snow boots over sockless feet. In my desperation, I refuse to spend time looking for socks. With the box of home movies in my arms, I quickly but carefully walk down the icy steps of our front porch and into the garage. This is where my brother's room is—the only place in my family home that still has a VCR.

Upon entering my brother's room, I gag from the musty smell of tobacco and alcohol. I push aside dirty laundry as I plop onto his sagging mattress in front of his old-fashioned television set.

After perusing the box of tapes, I settle on one labeled "Olivia's Birth." Olivia is my cousin (Aunt Susie's youngest daughter). I specifically remember my aunt telling me about the content of this video. It was the day of Olivia's birth, and my mother volunteered to record the whole afternoon in the delivery room.

My index finger trembling, I push the tape into the VCR and wait. It makes several clinking noises and hisses. I push the stop button and then rewind. I need this. *I eject the tape to see if the VCR has eaten it. Nope. After a few more minutes of maneuvering, I finally get the tape to play.*

I hold my breath, waiting for the moment I've been longing for.

In front of me is my cousin Olivia as a newborn in the hospital bassinet.

"Here's the babyyyy. . . Isn't she prrrettyyy?"

I inhale sharply.

It's Mom's voice.

Her voice sounds both familiar and foreign. I feel resonance with her voice, physically, in my gut. However, it sounds higher and much softer than I remember. Childlike. Perhaps she's trying to mimic the voice of the newborn, as she once did with our family dog. Perhaps I'm so used to the version of her voice in my imagination that her actual, real voice doesn't sound right. I try to let go of my uncertainty and not just hear her voice but feel it. When I do, it's like that first sip of water after a deep thirst. It's cooling. It's calming. I slowly savor every note of her voice.

There are a few moments of silence in the video and then a close-up of Olivia. The camera zooms out and focuses on Aunt Susie holding her newborn daughter.

Mom continues to narrate. "And her mom's lookin' like a fox, too!" Aunt Susie gives Mom a look of affectionate annoyance. It wouldn't be a true family event without my mother's humor.

I laugh through the tears that flow down my face.

Susie says to the camera, "Do you want to hold her, Ann?"

Mom hands the camera to someone else, and suddenly there she is. I can't believe my eyes. I haven't seen my mother in eight years, except in photographs that don't embody her loving, moving presence. Growing up, my mother gave my brother and me a lot of tough love, but she always provided us with the promise of tenderness. We were always guaranteed a soft pair of shoulders to fall into, filled with the smells of scented body cream and the texture of curly hair brushing against our faces.

I stare in wonder at my mother rocking my cousin Olivia in her arms. In this moment, I'm actually envious of Olivia. I want to feel my mom's touch. I want her to hold me in her arms again. I want to feel her warm, smooth lipstick brush against my cheek. I envy a baby—a baby who's a grown woman now. To soothe my frustration, I close my eyes and invite my body to remember the feeling of my mother's embrace.

In this moment, I realize that I do feel her embrace. I do hear her voice. I do continue a relationship with her.

And with this realization, I am free from the tyranny of closure.

THE RENDEZVOUS

* * *

What does it mean to hold on to letting go of the dead? A 2010 Randy Rogers Band song called "Holding on to Letting Go" might provide insight. In it, the singer laments a former lover. And yet he finds some comfort in grieving and reflecting on his memories of their relationship. The lyrics suggest potential ways of mourning the deceased. When loved ones die, can we ever truly let go of them and the memories they leave behind? Perhaps processes of holding on and letting go are not diametrically opposed. There may be ways to hold on to the memory and presence of the deceased while letting go of the more paralyzing aspects of grief and mourning.

Freud (1917/1961) argued that, regarding the bereavement process, "When the work of mourning is completed the ego becomes free and uninhibited again" (p. 245). Throughout his career, Freud revised his theories on grief. Even though he first described grief as the freeing of the ego, eventually he acknowledged that a connection with the deceased would remain after death (Berzoff, 2011). However, Freud never claimed that actively maintaining this connection would be healthy. After Freud's theoretical contributions, many scholars of the bereavement process built upon his work through psychological attachment theory (Bowlby, 1961; Kubler-Ross, 1969; Parkes, 1975; Worden, 1991). This scholarship led, in the United States, to a contemporary paradigm of grieving in which the bereaved can and should "recover" from grief by relinquishing ties with the deceased. Klass, Silverman, & Nickman (1996) challenged this perspective. They argued that though the deceased was no longer physically present, a relationship with that person could still be maintained. The bereaved could form "continuing bonds" with the deceased, and these relationships should not necessarily be deemed pathological.

Since the introduction of the continuing bonds paradigm, many researchers have conducted studies that have extended Klass, Silverman, and Nickman's foundational work (Berns, 2011; Biank & Werner-Lin, 2011; Clements, DeRanieri, & Benasutti, 2004; Davis, 2010; Ellis, 2013; Hedtke & Winslade, 2004; Klass et al., 1996; Parkes & Prigerson, 2010; Paxton, 2013, 2014; Rennels & Paxton, 2013; Valentine, 2008). Many of these scholars have offered strategies for the bereaved to construct a bond after death, including telling stories about those who have died, having conversations with the deceased, celebrating their birthdays and anniversaries, and reviewing artifacts that represent or once belonged to them. Hedtke & Winslade (2004) call these "re-membering" processes by which the deceased can regain active membership in their loved ones' lives. These practices are much more active than simply reminiscing about the dead and require engaging in behaviors that make the deceased's presence more apparent.

Apart from offering strategies for re-membering and continuing bonds, some scholars have compared the effectiveness of continuing bonds for individuals grieving different types of loss (e.g., gradual or unexpected) (Carr, House, Wortman, Nesse, & Kessler, 2001; Stroebe, Abakoumkin, Stroebe, & Schut, 2011). Other theorists have revealed how specific populations of the bereaved (e.g., widows and widowers, parents who have lost children, children who have lost parents) form continuing bonds (Bennett, 2010; Cacciatore & Flint, 2012; Kempson & Murdock, 2010; Tyson-Rawson, 1996). Researchers also have described how continuing bonds are formed differently among family members who experience the death of a loved one (Foster et al., 2011). In short, the idea of continuing bonds has been widely discussed and explored in various fields, including psychology, social work, gerontology, and more recently communication (Davis, 2010; Ellis, 2013; Paxton, 2013, 2014, 2017; Rennels & Paxton, 2013).

In order to effectively continue this research, scholars must consider the various ways grief can be discussed in any situation. As Neimeyer (2001) argues:

> There is no single 'grand narrative' of grief but a panoply of perspectives within which any given family or individual is positioned. Situated at the confluence of multiple discursive streams, each person constructs a unique response to bereavement that distills the meanings of loss current in his or her family, community, and culture. Each of these ways of 'languaging' about loss, in turn, provides a partial prescription for how loss is to be accommodated by the individual and the social world. Viewing bereavement within a discursive frame configures grief therapy as a rhetorical process, with rhetoric being understood as the artful use of language to achieve pragmatic ends.
>
> (p. 264)

Developing alternative ways of speaking about grief and relationships with the deceased can be important in helping bereaved individuals relearn their world (Attig, 2001). How might the process of continuing bonds with the deceased alter some of the discourses about grieving and our communicative practices for showing social support to the bereaved?

In attempting to answer this question, researchers may encounter many obstacles. People often cast grief as one of the ultimate villains in the story of human experience—as something to be defeated, resolved, or avoided. This view of grief seems to be more common in the United States than in other countries. In other countries, continuing a relationship with a deceased person is not considered eccentric, and citizens culturally allow one another more time to grieve a death. For example, in Mexico and other Latin countries the Day of the Dead is a celebration of the deceased's continued presence. However, often in the United States, when someone dies, individuals have several colloquial phrases to choose from when wanting to show support: "I'm sorry for your loss," "I know how you feel (or what you're going through)," or "He (or she) is in a better place." Consider the following alternative phrases: "I am here to listen and feel your grief," "Your loved one may be physically gone, but perhaps there are ways to connect with his (or her) continued presence," or "I am here to help you relearn your life throughout your indefinite grieving process." I do not believe many people in the United States are accustomed to hearing such phrases. Some bereaved individuals might even react negatively to them. However, I believe they are worth considering as additions to our ways of addressing grief and loss. As a communication scholar, I believe that introducing these alternative discourses can transform "feeling rules" for grief (Hochschild, 1983) and help the bereaved grieve well (Frank, 1991).

In this book, I explore these issues through ethnographic inquiry into a case study of my own continuing bonds. I try to understand the lived experience of continuing bonds, how they work, and how they can fail. Through writing academic papers, volunteering at a bereavement center, and teaching about continuing bonds in the classroom, I have embraced the possibility of my mother's ongoing presence in my life. These activities also have left me feeling more connected to those who are still living—even people whom I felt I had little in common with or a lack of purpose in having a relationship. So, this book explores not only how continuing bonds activities can make people feel closer to the deceased, but also how these bonds, rather than pulling people out of the world of the living, might facilitate stronger relationships with those who are still alive.

As with all paradigm shifts (Kuhn, 1962), some people still want to cling to the traditional grieving model based on detachment with the deceased. A few theorists argue that in some situations continuing bonds will make the bereavement process worse, encouraging the bereaved to form a co-dependent relationship with the deceased (Packman, Horsley, Davies, & Kramer, 2006). Klass (2006) has responded to these critiques by stating that when he and his colleagues developed the theory of continuous bonds it was not their intention to argue that it was a panacea for grieving. Rather, their goal was to develop a richer understanding of the bereavement process and to show that if an individual can maintain a healthy relationship with the deceased this should not be considered pathological. Klass writes, "My own position, then, has been that the criteria for the health of an interpersonal bond are the same whether the bond is between living people or between living people and dead people" (p. 845). There are cases in which a continuous bond can be unhealthy, especially if the relationship with the deceased was hostile or ambivalent before his or her death.

Furthermore, in this response to critics, Klass (2006) proposes that researchers of continuous bonds should start exploring more of their collective nature. While some research has been valuable, he argues, too much emphasis has been placed on the individual nature of continuous bonds: "If we do not include community, cultural, and political narratives in our understanding of continuing bonds we are in danger of using attachment theory to build bereavement theory that applies to a small portion of one population in one historical time" (p. 856). Culture influences the way in which communities form relationships and talk about grief. These communities and networks then inform the individual on how to treat the deceased. The individual can also influence the community's way of collectively continuing a bond.

Root & Exline (2014) expand on this notion of community influences. They argue:

> Because bereavement is not a solely internal experience, it is important to examine continuing bonds' interface with the "living community." Individuals who experience continuing bonds are parts of families, communities, societies, and cultures that may encourage or inhibit maintaining

connections with the deceased. . . If bereaved individuals are concerned that their continued ties to the deceased will be criticized or rejected by others, they may feel limited in their experiences of the bond or may find the bond distressing.

(p. 5)

They argue that the next step for researchers of continuing bonds is to study the bereaved individual's subjective experience of the continued bond expression and the bereaved person's interpretation of the meaning of the expression—"in particular, what the expression signifies about the bereaved, about the deceased, and about their relationship" (p. 5). To better understand this subjective experience of continuing a bond, they argue, researchers can also look at other factors, such as the relationship with the deceased before death and afterlife beliefs.

If family and community members accept the dead's ongoing presence in their lives, this may also change how they describe grief and loss. Does the loss of a loved one always have to be viewed as something we need to "get over"? Although I have felt sadness because I miss my mother's physical presence, I have found great joy in continuing a relationship with her after death. People often are encouraged to seek closure after the death of a loved one—even when the meanings of closure are contradictory and unclear (Berns, 2011). If we accept continuing bonds (rather than closure) as a guide for living after the death of a loved one, what does this look and feel like in everyday life? Can grief ever be satisfying (Sprengnether, 2002)? How does one experience grief in the best way possible?

In order to address these questions, I have analyzed my own experiences of continuing a relationship with my deceased mother and how this relationship has evolved over time. This required me to engage in meta-autoethnography—to review past autoethnographic projects (Paxton, 2013, 2014; Rennels & Paxton, 2013) I had done on the topic and also interrogate my current emotional experiences associated with the loss—and, as Ellis (2008) proposed, "turn narrative snapshots I have written in the past into a form more akin to a video—a text in motion—one in which I drag and drop in new experiences as well as revised interpretations of old storylines, then reorder and thus re-story them" (p. 13). Through my meta-autoethnographic analyses, I have found that the feelings I experienced with grief did not always coincide with societal prescriptions. Similar to what Ellis (1991) describes in her work on the sociological introspection of emotions, I sometimes felt culturally opposed emotions (such as joy and sadness) simultaneously. There were moments when grief empowered me to make better decisions in my life. I even desired and sought out experiences in which I knew I would grieve—not just alone but with others.

Since grieving is not only an individual but also a relational and communal process, I also explored the complexities of other people's stories about and emotional experiences with losing my mother. These individuals included family members and friends in my hometown community as well as new friends with whom I had shared my loss on an intimate level. To study this, I completed six weeks of ethnographic fieldwork in my hometown of DuQuoin, Illinois—conducting interactive interviews (Ellis, Kiesinger, & Tillman-Healy, 1997) with family members, my mother's close friends, and her salon clients. My hope was that this project would not solely be about feelings of grief but also explore how we all may find ways to live the best we can with grief. Furthermore, I wanted to show how the process of writing and sharing personal narratives can contribute to the process of continuing bonds and help us heal from trauma and disruption.

This book investigates how continuing a bond with the deceased is a relational, communicative, and communal phenomenon as well as an individual, internal, and psychological process. It expands the perspective on continuing bonds as a coping strategy to a narrative blueprint for living one's life. In writing this book, I have tried to address some of the experiential properties and "feeling rules" of grief and continuous bonding with loved ones who have died. For example, the canonical sense of sadness is that it is a negative emotion that one wants to get rid of. But, as Sprengnether (2002) writes, "Sadness, at some times and in some conditions, may be perceived as satisfying—if not blissful, then at least serious and grave, if not perfect or full, then at least enough" (p. 180). Those who want to continue talking about and incorporating the deceased in their daily lives will hopefully find resonance in my work. They will know that they are not alone, and that other people also cherish the moments in which grief can fill them up—making them feel more alive, whole, and engaged with life. It is possible to engage in the dialectical dance with the dead by holding on to letting go.

CHAPTER 1

GOODBYE[1]

It's a Monday morning, and I'm on winter break from school. Roused from sleep by the sound of my mother groaning and cursing, I jump from bed to find a familiar scene. My mother is plucking hair from her cheeks in front of the bathroom mirror.

"I'm a damn man-woman," she mutters. She squints and furrows her brow. Each pluck of the tweezers is more aggressive than the last—her anger escalating.

She pauses in her tweezing and stares at her reflection. Her disheveled hair frames a face full of fear. My mother likes to wear a lot of makeup. But in the early morning hour before she uses the cosmetics to cover her perceived flaws, I see the deep, dark circles under her eyes.

Noticing me watching her from the hallway, she turns to face me. She throws down the tweezers in the sink and shouts in frustration. "I just used the hair removal cream three fucking days ago! What the hell is going on?"

I shrug in reply. We have a unique relationship for a mother and a teenage son. Although I wouldn't say I tell my mother everything about my life, I do share a lot with her—my goal of being a famous writer, my frustrations at school, and my bowel movements. Personal boundaries in our relationship are sometimes so loose that I've even discussed a bowel movement with her while making one. My mother has jokingly coined

---

1 Portions of this chapter were previously published in *Qualitative Inquiry*, 2013, 19 (5): 355–365, and have been reproduced with permission from Sage Publications.

the phrase "having a blaster" for particular occasions in the restroom, and this has caught on among our family members and friends. I'm glad we can share a giggle over these types of issues, but it saddens me when I see her body causing her so much frustration.

She washes and dries her face, tightens the front of her red bathrobe, and walks out of the bathroom to meet me in the hallway. "Between this shit and the swelling and the weight gain and the headaches, I'm losing my mind!"

My mother has struggled with weight issues for most of her life. "If only I could get back to that weight!" she has said numerous times when reviewing her wedding photographs. She was only 18 when she and my father married, and back then she possessed a smaller, lighter frame. I often wonder why she likes to look at these old pictures. Does she feel so much shame about her body that it's a way for her to relive her moments as a thinner woman? I think Mom is beautiful no matter what size she is, and I wish she could understand that about herself. There are so many times I've been saddened when watching her put herself down.

These moments of self-deprecation have become worse over the last three months. For some reason, Mom has been rapidly gaining weight—even with no change in her diet. This isn't normal weight gain either, because she is retaining water. "I'm the fucking Michelin man," she's been telling people. My mother likes to joke, but as I stare at her bare swollen ankles this morning, the situation doesn't seem funny.

"Come on. Let me fix you some breakfast," she says. "We're not going to be able to do this for long, because you're going back to school soon."

On our way to the kitchen she peeks into my younger brother's bedroom. "Let's not wake the sleeping dead," she murmurs.

Our house is unusually quiet with my father at work and my brother sleeping. I cherish such times when Mom and I are alone together. As we walk into the kitchen and look out the back window, we're surprised to see a thick blanket of snow on the ground.

"All right! Look at that!" My mother exclaims. She loves snow as much as I do. She also is fascinated with snow globes and snowmen—a tall curio cabinet in our living room houses her many treasures.

The temporary serenity of the morning is abruptly interrupted when Maddie, our pet beagle, shoots into the kitchen—her claws create a clicking symphony across the hardwood floor. She charges to the glass door leading into the backyard and begins growling menacingly.

I softly stroke the back of her neck and ask, "What is it, girl?"

And then I spot a bright flash of red. There's a cardinal slowly prancing across the ground.

Mom opens the door to let Maddie out, explaining "I don't want her to wake up your brother."

We both laugh as Maddie dodges through the snow toward the cardinal. She looks like a clumsy puppet on a string, running and then collapsing to the ground. The cardinal quickly spots her and flies away.

Mom murmurs, "Dumb-ass dog. She'll be whimpering to come back inside within five minutes. What do you bet?"

"Yep," I respond as I take a seat at our kitchen table. I can tell we haven't kept the heat on very high during the night when I feel the cool press of the wooden seat underneath my boxers. I shiver and pull my hands into the sleeves of my shirt.

"So what's for breakfast, Mom?"

She smiles and opens the refrigerator door. "Well, you are in luck, mister. While you were out at the movies last night, I rolled out some donut holes!"

Yes! Mom's homemade fried donut holes. This will be a perfect treat for the cool winter morning. The idea of the hot sugary dough melting in my mouth already makes me feel warmer.

As I peruse the local newspaper, I watch Mom in action. She places the pan of raw donut holes on the counter next to the stove. Then she heats a pot of oil and turns on the radio. Her eyes light up when she hears one of her favorite tunes, "Perfect," by country singer Sara Evans. During the introductory section of the song, I giggle as she starts shaking her hips back and forth with the spatula raised over her head.

She begins tossing the raw dough into the oil, and as each one crackles it creates a nice accompaniment to the song. The smell of fried goodness massages my nostrils and makes my stomach growl more strongly. By the time my mother reaches the song's chorus, I join in.

I try to push aside my worries about Mom and just enjoy the moment. We don't get to spend as much quality time together as we would like to, because she works a lot. She has her own salon in our home, and you might think this would help her spend more time with my brother and me. But she's a popular hairdresser with a long list of clients, and if those clients don't make their next appointment before they leave the salon, they can expect to wait at least six weeks before seeing her again.

The stress from work also has not helped her feel better about whatever's going on with her body. I tell myself that everything will be fine. I tell myself that it's probably just a "female" problem—an issue with her hormones. I tell myself just to sing along and have fun with Mom.

But I can't help but worry about her strange situation, and I hate that she feels so unattractive and like a freak.

I can relate in some ways. I know what it's like to feel different.

* * *

I watch Mark run.

It's a steamy afternoon in late April, and I'm waiting for jazz band practice to begin. Our high school's graduation ceremony is approaching, and I'm one of the lucky few underclassmen who will have the opportunity to play during commencement. Usually, I feel a certain comfort with my baritone saxophone. The feel of the cool, smooth metal beneath my fingertips is a signal that moments of joy and creation are imminent. But my thoughts are far away from music right now. I grip the saxophone closer to my chest and continue watching Mark from a nearby window.

Mark is one of the seniors who'll be graduating this spring, and he's on the track team. At my high school, the football field and surrounding track are close by the band room. It is often difficult for students to be both in the jazz band and on the track team, because practices meet at the same time. *Oh well. It's not like my fat butt can run anyway.*

I tend to not get along with most of the "jocks" at school, because they're often arrogant. They like to make fun of me because I'm heavy and a geek. My mother mockingly calls them "cool dudes" in an exaggeratedly husky, masculine voice. "You just keep doing what you're doing in school. Don't worry about the cool dudes," she often tells me.

Mark is different from the other "cool dudes." He's a nice guy. I have known him ever since I started high school, because his locker is only two away from mine. On day one of my first year, I was panicking because I could not get my locker open, and he helped me unjam it. From that point on, we have spoken to each other just about every day. Every time football season is about to begin, he tries to get me to join the team. "Dude, you've got the shape and size of a lineman. You'd be killer on the field!"

I do have the body type for a football star, but I don't have enough of a desire to play. The idea of trying to tackle someone and people trying to tackle me is terrifying. This breaks not only Mark's heart but also my father's.

Mark and I don't run in the same circle of friends, so we haven't spent much time together outside of school. It would probably be social suicide for him to be seen with me. Mark is tall and handsome, with broad shoulders and large biceps. He's also one of those guys who can pull off a buzz cut.

As I watch him run around the football field, I also notice his legs. *Boy, does he have really nice . . . I mean built . . . legs. They're tan, with just the right amount of hair. And wow. What awesome bulging calves and thick thighs. . .*

His track shorts are high up enough on his waist that I can also see a smooth, white tan line peeking out from beneath each leg opening. The air is on full blast in the band room, but I feel a bead of sweat roll down my forehead.

That's hot.

What? Why did you just think that?

A conflicting self-dialogue sets my mind racing.

Okay. It's not "hot." Maybe that's not the right word.

Are you gay?

NO!

You were definitely checking out his legs.

So? . . . That doesn't make me gay. I can appreciate another man's physique. Maybe I want my legs to look like his.

Faggot!

Shut up!

It's true. Don't you feel your boner right now?

I had that before I started watching Mark. It's because I talked with my friend Sarah on the way to practice.

Whatever. Your friend Sarah—who's a girl! Who's one of your many GIRL-FRIENDS. Gay guys have lots of friends who are girls.

That's just a stereotype.

You want Mark to touch you. . .

STOP!

The band director taps her baton against the podium and my troubling thoughts are silenced. I begin to play the opening stanza of the first concert piece, but I can't help but continue to feel a strange mix of desire and dread.

And with every resting measure of the song, I continue to glance out the window.

* * *

DuQuoin, my hometown, is a small, rural community in southern Illinois with about six thousand residents. When most people in the country think of Illinois, they think of Chicago. Although Chicago is a notable major metropolis of the United States, it does not represent the whole state of Illinois. Some individuals have argued that the northern and southern regions of Illinois are so different that they could be separate states. The boundary between northern and southern Illinois is also difficult to decipher. Most people claim that any community below Interstate 80 is considered southern territory. Others say that any place south of Champaign is considered southern territory. Some argue that the state is divided into three geographic regions: northern, southern, and central Illinois.

Southern Illinois has a distinct culture. The physical environment is filled with farmland and cornfields. The roads are long, winding, and often hilly. There are urban aspects of the communities, which often include many subdivisions and historic town squares.

DuQuoin is no exception. Along Main Street, there is a town square with various small businesses: post office, local bakery, movie theater, banks, shoe store, T-shirt store, antiques and collectibles store, gas stations, bars, restaurants, and one of the town's many Christian churches. The larger business chains (including Wal-Mart and fast-food restaurants) are located farther south in the town. Even farther south is a section of small ponds and rolling hills known as the DuQuoin State Fairgrounds. Every August for two weeks, the town hosts a fair with carnival rides, food stands, and a lineup of music shows in beer tents and a small stadium. This stadium, known as the DuQuoin Grandstand, is where a circus is held every fall and where all school graduations take place.

When the fair is not in session, residents use the grounds for walking and running exercise. Families fish and have picnics. Children often feed ducks in the ponds. A monthly flea market and different programs are held at a large exhibition hall located in the grounds. During the winter months, there is a Christmas light exhibit that residents leisurely drive through and observe from their cars. When school is canceled because of winter weather, many students find a way to drive to the grounds and spend the day sledding down the hills.

My mother and father were born and raised in DuQuoin. Most of their siblings still reside here too. Not everyone continues to reside in the town when they graduate high school, but many residents stay in the general area of southern Illinois. The nearest university is about 30 minutes away, and often town residents will commute to school. Although I appreciate the comfort of small-town life and the friendly personalities of my fellow residents, I hope to leave DuQuoin after graduating high school.

* * *

"Maddie, get down!" my Grandma Jo-Ann yells. Grandma is eating a chocolate-chip cookie from Hardee's, and our dog Maddie is jumping on her lap attempting to get a piece. Jo-Ann's hair appointment has been finished for at least an hour, but she has decided to visit with her daughter during work hours.

It's a humid spring afternoon. I sit in my mother's salon and watch the chaotic scene. Although the environment is hectic, I still believe that my mother's salon (the "Hair Loft," as she calls it) has a Southern charm similar to the beauty shop in *Steel Magnolias.* Mom serves mostly female clientele, elderly women and mothers. They chatter avidly about the latest small-town gossip—from who's expecting to who's having an affair to who's being forced to close their small business. The salon is adjacent to the kitchen, in what used to be our garage. My father has built a separate building that now serves as the garage, next to our house. When he first finished building it, my mother rolled her eyes and said, "The damn garage looks bigger than our house." Even though it isn't larger than our house, for some reason it appears that way.

Working at home has its advantages and disadvantages. My mother does not have to commute to work, but the line between work and home seems blurry at times. Family and friends sometimes have the impression that even though my mother works certain days and times of the week, she might make exceptions for them. As kind as my mother is, I hate that she has a lot of difficulty saying no to these requests.

Her father, my Grandpa Corky, has been dead for two years now, but I often laugh about a special memory of him in the salon. Grandpa was a cheerful and chubby man, but he liked to stay active to try to combat his diabetes. When he was bored and wasn't playing golf, he would often go to a nearby mall. He would go there not to shop but to exercise and to flirt with some of the younger female cashiers. When I went to the mall with him, he would introduce me to some of these women. As a big flirt, he was conscious about his age, so he tried to make himself appear younger. My mother would color his hair to cover up the gray. It was like a secret operation: he would only let her do it after hours, with the blinds drawn. What makes me chuckle is how Mom would sometimes have to distract an unexpected visitor from coming into the salon during these secret appointments. Grandpa would pace back and forth, the black color smeared around his temples, while my mother stood outside the door creating quick diversions.

My sweet reverie is interrupted when my younger brother, Kyle, comes crashing through the salon door drenched in mud. My mother looks up from cutting a young female client's hair and yells, "KYLE! What the hell have you been doing?"

Kyle replies, "I've been riding my four-wheeler."

Mom turns to him in exasperation and points her scissors at him. "Go straight to the laundry room and put those in the wash!"

"You are such a dumb-ass dog!" my grandma yells as Maddie continues to beg.

Mom shoots grandma a look of annoyance—a look that says she should leave—but my grandmother ignores it. My grandmother assumes she deserves special treatment after raising seven children.

As my brother retreats into the laundry room, my father comes through the salon door. "Now, come on, girl! You can't be misbehaving like that!" He laughs flirtatiously. I look behind him to see Mom's hair-product salesperson, Christine—a sassy redhead who always gets my father's attention.

Christine chuckles and asks my mother, "How the hell do you put up with this one?" She takes a seat next to another female client who is sitting under a hair dryer getting a permanent. My mother has become somewhat of a contortionist, with the ability to serve several clients at once. Often, she'll do a quick haircut while another person is sitting under the dryer getting a perm or highlights. This usually goes well, but it can turn disastrous. If a customer takes too long discussing a haircut or for some reason it takes longer than expected to color a client's hair, there's a catastrophic domino effect. The next scheduled customer arrives, the salon gets even more crowded, and my mother feels the crushing pressure of economic responsibility and of upholding her great reputation as a local hairdresser.

Mom turns to Christine and responds, "I threaten to withhold sex."

Everyone in the salon bursts out laughing. The dog continues to bark and beg for Grandma's cookie. I place my head in my hands and shake it back in forth with exaggerated embarrassment. My mother is known for her talent as a hairdresser, but many of her clients also describe the entertainment you'll most likely receive during your appointment.

The phone rings and Mom answers: "Hair Loft. Ann speaking." She attempts to cradle the phone between her shoulder and ear while cutting her client's hair. I look around at the pandemonium and wonder how she keeps her sanity.

* * *

"I have a tumor."

My mother utters the words, and my heart wants to leap out of my chest. She and my father exchange a troubled glance and look back at Kyle and me. We've just finished dinner and are sitting in the living room.

I had hoped that what was happening to Mom was just a hormonal problem—a condition that could be remedied with some medication. But a tumor? This is a big deal.

"Where is it?" I ask, but I'm wondering about so many other things too. *Can the doctor remove it? If so, what does the surgery entail? Will my mom be able to be the same great mom she has always been? Is the tumor cancerous?* And the most excruciating question of them all: *Could Mom die from this?*

Mom lets out a deep breath and continues, "The tumor is in my pituitary gland, which is located at the base of the skull."

Oh my god, it's in her head!

"My endocrinologist, Dr. Clark, says that this is often referred to as the master gland. It controls most of your body's hormones. The tumor is causing my body to produce too much of a hormone called ACTH. This is why I have been having problems with weight gain and hair growth. These are also symptoms of a condition called Cushing's disease. When people have this type of tumor, the disease often accompanies it."

Kyle interrupts, "You have a disease?"

My father places one hand on my mother's shoulder and jabs a cautionary finger in the air. "Just listen to your mother," he advises.

Mom shifts uncomfortably on the sofa. "I only have the disease when the tumor is present. The good news is that the tumor can be removed. Your dad and I are going to see a neurosurgeon in St. Louis next week to discuss my options."

St. Louis, Missouri, the nearest major city, is about ninety miles away. There is a hospital in our town, but any time anyone discusses going to the hospital in St. Louis it means the condition is serious. I feel the hairs stand up on the back of my neck and the slight hint of worried tears. *When will Mom ever get a break?*

This isn't the first health problem she has encountered. Four years ago, she kept feeling sharp pains in her stomach. They were so painful she would have to quit work for the day and lie down. Doctors diagnosed her pains as stomach polyps, and she had them surgically removed. A year later, she tore a meniscus in her knee. Six weeks after the surgery to fix her knee, she developed a blood clot and had to be rushed to the hospital via ambulance.

She had survived these challenges, and I thought this was enough. *My mom is a good person. Why the hell does God keep giving her all of this shit to deal with?* I keep thinking about all of my friends and *their* moms. I never hear about *them* having health problems. Maybe they do, and they keep this information from their children. I also think about some of the students who torture me every day at school. Why can't *their* moms get sick? And then I feel guilty for wishing illnesses on their mothers. Nobody deserves what my mother has had to go through.

"We don't want to keep anything from you boys," my father says. "It is just important that you are good for your mom. Keep up with your chores and be nice. We'll get through this." He gives Mom's hand a tight squeeze.

"So you're going to keep working?" I ask Mom.

"Yes. I don't see the point in quitting until the surgery. If my headaches get too painful, I may have to take the day off. I'm trying to spread the word to my clients as quickly as I can."

18

There's a moment of silence among the four of us, and then Mom asks, "Is there anything else you want to talk about?"

Kyle and I shake our heads and retreat to his room, where we keep the Super Nintendo. We both grab our controls and plop on the floor in front of the television to play our game—*Super Donkey Kong*. The game's main players are two monkeys that throw bananas at opponents and ride on train tracks in wobbly carts. I try to concentrate on the game, but I'm distracted by what our mother has said. Kyle and I play in silence, with the weight of illness bearing down upon us.

Kyle pauses the game.

He turns to me in a panic. "Mom is going to be okay . . . right?"

I begin to respond but then hesitate. What is my role as the older brother? Do I show him my fears? Do I tell him that I too worry about her surgery, cancer, and even possible death?

No. I do what I've been taught, compartmentalize my emotions, and sternly say, "Of course. She's going to be fine."

My gut tells me otherwise.

* * *

My mother's surgery is successful—for the most part. Her surgeon, Dr. Grayson, has to microscopically go through her nose to remove the tumor. Unfortunately, the tumor is so close to the optic nerve that he can't remove it all, because he fears this would blind her. She now must continue radiation therapy to shrink the tumor every week at the hospital in St. Louis. This requires a three-hour round-trip. I'm too young to drive in the city, and my brother can't drive yet. My father is busy working and trying to support our family while also keeping our health insurance to pay for my mother's medical expenses. Luckily, with the help of her four sisters, friends, neighbors, and various clients from her hair salon, my mother is able to go for her radiation treatments.

* * *

"Well hellooooo Dolly. Well hello—Dolly! It's so nice to have you back where you belong," I proudly bellow the refrain of the song. Even with the heat of the stage lights, with the sweat rolling down my face and smearing my makeup, and with my whole body fatigued from dancing, singing, and making costume changes for the last two hours, I could do this all night. I look out at the dark sea of faces in the audience. I can't recognize anyone, but I know Mom is there.

Every summer, I'm involved in a community theater group that is run by two local music teachers. The group organizes two different shows every season—one for children and young adults (8–14 years old) and the other for adults (15 years and older). I have performed in the shows every summer since I was in the fourth grade, and my mother has been a huge supporter of these activities. She has helped me prepare for every audition, carpooled with my friends' mothers getting us to every practice, and assembled my costumes and even put on my stage makeup. Even with her busy work schedule, she still volunteers to help backstage for some of the shows and dress rehearsals.

It doesn't matter how large or small my role in the show, she watches every performance she can. "When you get famous, don't forget your mother," she says. This year's role in *Hello, Dolly!* is much smaller than the one I had the previous year. I starred as the cowardly lion in *The Wizard of Oz*. In this show, I'm in the chorus acting as a server in a restaurant and a local community member of the city. This role requires more costume changes and less stage time. It's quite different from tromping around in a large fur suit and singing about courage, but I'm still having a lot of fun.

I think I enjoy theater more because I'm supported in my pursuits. This is the last show of the season, and most of my family members have already seen me perform. It's a bittersweet moment for many reasons. I'm sad because I won't see many of my friends in the show until next summer—some of them I may never see again. The cast will tear down the set tomorrow, and then we'll all go our separate ways. These thoughts run through my mind as the show comes to an end and I prepare to greet other actors and audience members backstage.

About 10 minutes pass and almost half the audience has exited. *That's strange. I'm sure Mom had a good seat tonight.* I look around the bathrooms. *Maybe she had to leave early to relieve herself.* She still hasn't appeared. I know she watched the show, because she was my ride here.

"Blake!"

I turn to see Susan, the mother of one of my friends in the show. She approaches me and gives me a hug. "Nice job tonight, bud! I think that was your best performance of the season!" Her enthusiasm quickly diminishes to subdued concern and continues, "Your mom had to leave after intermission."

I tense. "Oh? Is she okay?"

"She said her vision was bothering her, and it made her sick. I am going to give you a ride home."

Sensing my worry, Susan continues, "I guess she needs to get her prescription checked. That's all."

"Right."

* * *

The tumor continues to grow quickly—much faster than Mom's doctors expected. As it grows, it tortures my mother by causing her to see everything in double. She copes with this ailment by keeping one of her eyes closed throughout the day. In her usual fashion, she makes light of the situation and jokes about considering an eye patch and looking like a pirate.

My family worries about her going blind. I feel that there are some things we already refuse to see.

* * *

My mother screams in pain, as if she's being burned alive. It's one of the most frightening sounds I've ever encountered. I'm sure she has heard my agonizing screams of pain as a child, but they were probably nothing like this. Having the roles of parent and child switch feels like watching a mirror fall and shatter; you stand and stare hopelessly at the pieces, unable to reassemble them. You want to so badly, because that mirror helps you remain confident in who you both are and how things are supposed to be.

Not like this.

It's a Saturday afternoon. My mother usually works on Saturdays, but she has canceled all of her appointments because she can't tolerate the pain that radiates through her body. For the last three weeks, my mother has felt aches and pains—mostly in her back. She has described the sensation as similar to that of being continually gouged by small knives. Some days the pain has been so intense my forty-year-old mother has had to use a walker to get around the house. Time seems to have sped way too many years into the future, as I've watched her trudge up and down the hall from the living room to the bathroom, the intensity of the pain causing her to shake as she slowly moves with the walker. Her doctors are mystified as to why this is occurring, and she has been scheduling appointments for the last week to run more tests. In the meantime, they've prescribed pain medication, which has helped somewhat, except for days like this.

Grandma Jo-Ann, Aunt Cindy, and our neighbor Karen are in the living room, looking at one another in panic. My mother is reclined in the armchair, clutching one side of her back, then the other. "Oh . . . Fuck!" she yells.

"When was the last time she had any pain medicine?" Karen asks.

"I don't know, but I am going to call the hospital. She has got to see one of those doctors. *Today*," Cindy insists.

"I'm not going to that goddamn place today! I can't! I hurt too much," Mom sobs.

Grandma walks over to my mother's side and attempts to calm her. She turns back to Cindy and Karen says, "You might want to call John in case we need some help from the men."

I overhear Cindy urging her husband, John, to come to our house. I consider contacting my father at work, but I stand paralyzed watching this train wreck in front of me. Kyle is riding his four-wheeler around the neighborhood, and I'm thankful that he's not being subjected to this. But why should *I* have to witness this anguish?

My anger at God is overshadowed by fear when my mother yells out in intensified pain. My heart jumps in my chest, and I feel tears form in my eyes. The emotions I feel are a strange mix: sadness because my mother is in pain, numbness because I'm in shock, anxiety because I feel this strong desire for her to get to a hospital as quickly as possible, and compassion because I want to hug her. Just as a mother kisses her child to ease the pain of scrapes and bruises, I want to do the same.

But I can't, because whatever is causing her pain is invisible and underneath the skin, and it's so powerful even strong pain medication can't soothe it. All I can do is stare and pray.

From the kitchen, I can hear my Aunt Cindy raging on the phone. "She has to see someone, *today*! Yes, her surgeon is Dr. Michael Grayson . . . I already told you what medication she is on!"

Within minutes my uncle and Karen's husband have arrived. They get ready to lift my mother off the chair and she yells, "You guys are not going to be able to get my fat ass off this chair!"

I sigh. Even in the worst conditions, she tries to make a feeble joke.

She continues to yell and resist the men's attempts to hold on to her. "I can't go! It just hurts too much. There's . . . no . . . way!"

GOODBYE

Karen leans over the arms of the chair and sternly speaks face-to-face with Mom. "Ann! Look here. Look at me! I know you hurt, but we have to figure out what is going on with you. We're going to get you to St. Louis. Maybe they can prescribe you something stronger, but you are going to have to tough this out. Don't just do it for you. Don't do it for us. Do it for your boys."

Mom looks up from the chair at me. In our exchange, I see desperation in her eyes. I can't imagine the things running through her mind. Maybe seeing me gives her a temporary burst of strength, and I can at least help in that way. By seeing me, maybe she's reminded of one of the many reasons she needs to live.

The next few minutes seem to move in slow motion. Both men are able to maneuver my mother out of the chair. While my grandmother hugs me tightly, we watch Aunt Cindy and Karen help them guide Mom slowly out the front door, down the steps, and into my aunt and uncle's jeep.

As I watch them pull away, I wonder whether she'll return cured of her pain.

If not, will she ever be without pain again?

* * *

"I'm sorry. We don't know when she will be back to work," I say before hanging up the phone.

I look at Mom, who's sleeping in the armchair, with the walker still by her side. It's been two days since my aunt and uncle rushed her to the emergency room. Her neurosurgeon was flabbergasted as to what was causing her so much pain. He ended up prescribing her more pain medication and scheduling an MRI. Now, instead of what should be a peaceful quiet after the intensity of the storm, I experience an ominous stillness. The uncertainty of my mother's future lingers, and unanswered questions continue to weigh on the family. We're still waiting on the results of her MRI. Obviously, she can't work, and I've volunteered to notify her customers of her indefinite leave. They are all concerned about her.

I find myself becoming a useless source of information. I have to cover up uncertainties with forced optimism. I really want to say the following statements: "I don't know when she will be able to come back to work." "I don't know if she will feel better soon." "I don't know if she will ever be her normal self again." But, I offer what optimistic family members are

23

supposed to say: "We know she will get through this." "We're hoping for the best in her time of recovery." "We'll keep you updated on her results."

"And yes, I will let you know if we need anything," I respond at the end of every phone call, even though I know that no one can give us—give *her*—what she needs.

* * *

"So what did the doctor say?" I ask Mom and Dad.

It's a Sunday evening, and our family is enjoying an amazing dinner. My mother is usually the cook of the family, but due to her illness, my father has taken over many of these responsibilities. With his experience in formerly running a restaurant, he does well. He likes to grill meat the most. Tonight's dinner consists of pork chops, baked potato, and a side salad.

Since Mom is still in a lot of pain, we eat together in the living room. I make sure to heavily douse my salad and potato with fattening condiments. I'm not much of a fan of the pork chop, because I don't like fat on meat. If I even taste the slightest hint of fat, I'll gag. Mom usually will cut all the fat off every piece of meat. But this time I don't want to bother my mother or hear my father complain, so I force myself to eat my pork chop—fat and all.

We sit in front of the television in silence. Our Sunday dinners are usually relaxing and something I look forward to. Tonight is different. I have a feeling that an uninvited visitor may come bursting into our home at any minute.

I know Mom's neurologist called yesterday. While Dad was doing yard work and she was asleep, I snuck into their bedroom and listened to a message on their answering machine. "Hi. This is Dr. Grayson. We have Ann's results. Please call me back at your earliest convenience." Of course, I couldn't tell the nature of the news from the tone of his voice. Most doctors have probably perfected the act of sounding neutral. Although I had appreciated his professionalism, I secretly wished to hear a hint of positivity in the message.

And so, after finishing dinner, I continue to reflect on the news my parents might be giving us tonight. With mixtures of pork, barbeque sauce, butter, salt, sour cream, ranch dressing, bacon bits, croutons, and cheese, my stomach growls warnings of future indigestion. My nerves aren't helping, either. *How does it usually work in legal trials? Is the verdict more likely to be not guilty if the jury is out for a longer period of time? Or is it the other way around?* I realize that this is our family and not a court of law. The verdict will not be guilty or not guilty but rather news about the next hurdle we have to face in helping my mother get well.

The program we're watching has come to an end. When my father switches off the television, I know the moment I've been waiting for has arrived. I fight the urge to throw up.

"Your mom and I have to talk to you boys," he says. His expression is grim.

Mom looks nervous. "Now, Lindon. Do we really need to—"

"Yeah, Ann. We already talked about this."

Mom sighs. "You're right."

I look at Kyle. Glancing down at his dinner plate, he slowly forks through his leftover baked potato.

Dad continues, "Dr. Grayson called yesterday, and he gave us some news about your mom . . . about why she's having all of this pain throughout her body. So . . . you remember that they couldn't remove all of her pituitary tumor because it was too close to the optic nerve and other important parts of the brain?"

We nod, showing that we understand.

"He thought the radiation would shrink the tumor enough to where she would just have to have yearly checkups. Well, your mother's tumor has spread through her body . . . and it's cancerous."

I feel bile come up and burn my throat. I swallow it back down. Suddenly, one of my worst fears has become a reality. Aunt Betty and Grandpa Corky both died from lung cancer. Grandpa Lindell died from cancer of the esophagus. I've experienced family members dying from cancer before, but I never imagined Mom could get cancer. Nobody ever prepares you for these things.

Mom quickly takes over explaining the news. "So, I have been diagnosed with pituitary cancer. It's extremely rare."

The room suddenly begins spinning, and my breathing becomes labored.

"What does that mean?" I manage to choke out. *You are going to die?*

Mom answers, "Because few people have this cancer, Dr. Grayson is not sure what to expect. However, he said I should start chemotherapy. We've already scheduled my first treatment in two weeks."

Kyle shifts uncomfortably next to me on the sofa. "Will you lose your hair?" he asks.

Mom takes a tissue from her pocket and wipes her face. "Yes," she responds. "Come here, guys."

Kyle and I walk to my mother, and we embrace in a group hug. As she cries softly into my shoulder, I stroke her curly brown hair. In this moment, I try to be optimistic. *People beat cancer every day. Mom has gone through so much already . . . She surely can get through this last battle. We just have to keep praying.*

But as much as I try to reassure myself with these thoughts and put on a sturdy façade, I can't deny that I'm more scared than I've ever been.

* * *

It's now six days before Christmas. I'm working part-time as a cook in a family-owned Italian restaurant called Alongi's. It's nice to have the extra money, and the job helps keep my mind off of worries about Mom. I've worked here the last two years, and even though the tasks can be physically and emotionally exhausting, I have fun with my co-workers.

All of the cooks are male except for one female who works during the day. Most of the servers are female. The cooks, some of whom also go to school with me, are a rowdy bunch. They like to play practical jokes. Between shenanigans like hiding pizza toppings, throwing flour on one another, and wet-towel-snapping matches, I wonder how we ever get anything done. I also have learned the difficult lesson about what can happen when you disclose private information. My secret infatuation with a young woman named Melissa was leaked to all the cooking staff, and they took advantage of this information when she decided to show up at the drive-through to pick up food one evening. The men working during that shift decided to sing the Allman Brothers Band's "Sweet Melissa" in the background while I was waiting on her.

Today, aside from the old '80s rock music on the radio, there's an eerie silence in the kitchen. My co-workers haven't played any jokes, nor have they said much to me in general. I've only told a few close friends about my mother's diagnosis, but information gets around very quickly in a small town. I feel a strange mix of anger and gratitude when they look at me with pity. I want to yell, "Don't feel sorry for me! My mom is going to be fine!" But I realize that cancer represents a terrible scenario in most people's minds.

I look up from my station at the digital clock on the wall and realize my shift has ended. Tossing the last pizza of the night into the fiery-hot oven, I grab a paper towel and wipe sweat from my brow. I say to my co-worker, "Time to get the hell out of this joint." He nods at me, smiling. "Later, Paxton."

I untie my apron and toss it into the laundry bin on my way out the door. The pungent smell of garlic still clings to my skin. Normally the cool winter air would feel like a sharp slap in the face, but because of my five-hour shift in the kitchen heat, the cool feels wonderful. It signals soothing relief from the end of hard labor.

On the drive home, I jam out to some of my favorite country songs. I'm happy to be on winter break from school, and I'm looking forward to starting an internship in the spring at our city hall. I'm also worried about the future. The typical questions of a graduating high school senior are on my mind. *Where will I get into school? How will I afford it? Will my parents be able to help out?*

I pull into my driveway and am surprised to see an unfamiliar vehicle. I go in the house and find Randy and my father frantically standing over my mother. She's lying back in the armchair, shaking her head and moaning. Randy, a nurse, is a family friend.

My father shows a look of desperation mixed with relief when he sees me. "Blake, can you go to the store? Your mother's blood-pressure reader needs new batteries. Get size AAA."

I stand there staring in fear at the scene.

"Blake!" my father snaps. "I need you to go now!"

"Is everything all right?"

"Yes. Your mother is not feeling very well, and Randy has come over to check on her. But we need to take her blood pressure. Please go to the store."

I speed to the store. After unsuccessfully searching for the right battery size, I ask a clerk to assist me. As she slowly looks through the shelves, I want to scream at her to hurry the fuck up. After what feels like a hundred years, she hands me the batteries.

There are two people in front of me at the register. I think about asking to go ahead of them, but by the time I make the decision to ask it's already my turn to pay.

I rush home to find the situation has become worse. I'm paralyzed with fear, and I can hardly breathe when I see my mother lying unconscious on the floor and Randy giving her CPR. My dad is frantically talking on the phone to an ambulance dispatcher. He places his hand over the receiver and yells to me, "Blake, take your brother and the dog and stay in your room."

I want to help. I want to do something. But what can I do? I guide my younger brother, Kyle, into my bedroom while tugging Maddie's collar. Once we enter, Maddie paws and whines at the door. I pace back and forth. My heart feels like it's going to beat out of my chest. I start to feel dizzy, and the room begins to sway.

"Is Mom going to be okay?" Kyle asks.

"Yeah," I lie. "She's had a scare before. Remember, a couple years ago?" I'm referring to the time she had the blood clot in her knee. An ambulance had to take her to the hospital, but she ended up being okay. I pray, I *beg* to God for this time to be the same.

I'm startled from my thoughts by the shrill sounds of an ambulance outside our house. I watch out the window as workers place my mom on a stretcher, get into the ambulance, and drive away. My dad follows them in his car.

At this point, many of our neighbors are inside the house or standing in our front yard. Karen and Jon approach us. Karen says, "Do you guys want to go to the hospital? We can take you."

"Do you think we should go?" I ask.

"It's up to you." But I can tell from her concerned expression and the feeling of dread in my gut that I should go.

When we get into the emergency waiting room, I see familial pandemonium. All of my mother's siblings and my grandmother are there. Some are talking on their cell phones. Others are sitting in chairs and hugging one another. Their faces are filled with terrible worry.

Everyone's attention is drawn to the doctor as he emerges from the operating room. His expression is grim. My grandmother and one of my aunts rush to him and ask, "How is she?"

Everything comes to a halt. My world stops when he says, "I'm sorry. She didn't make it. We tried everything we could."

A cold numbness spreads through my body. I take in the sounds of agonizing moans from my relatives. Aunt Cindy slams her fist against the wall in frustration and yells, "God damn it! Why her? Why did you have to take her from us?" Tears of anger run down her face as she places her hand over her mouth, stifling a series of sobs.

The doctor asks, "Where are her children? They may see her at this time."

28

GOODBYE

My uncle gives me a tight squeeze on the shoulder and guides Kyle and me to the doctor. I feel as though this is just a horrible nightmare, and I'll eventually wake up. However, when I enter the room of my mother's death, and I see her lying on the exam table, I know this is all too real.

My father's head is buried in his arms draped over her. He looks up at Kyle and me. His eyes are flaring red, bloodshot. "Come here, guys," he murmurs.

I stand there, numbness continuing to radiate throughout my body. I look at this thing in front of me. This isn't my mother. The carefree, fun-loving woman who I know is not this post-mortem specimen. This corpse.

I snatch Kyle's hand as he tries to reach out and touch her. I tell myself it's to protect him, but it's really because if he touches her this will become more real for him and threaten to become a part of *my* reality. And this can't be happening.

We hug my father as he cries. I'm still in shock. The tears aren't coming yet, but they will. "She's in a better place now," my father assures us. "She won't feel pain any longer."

I slowly reach out and massage her thick, brown curls of hair—the only part of her that hasn't changed.

* * *

I lay flat on my back in bed, staring at the ceiling. Maybe if I focus all of my attention on the little white sparkles that scatter the white space, I can tune out the moans coming from the living room. Numbness continues to encapsulate my body. I can't move, nor do I want to. Maybe I'll just stay here, starve myself, and join Mom in the afterlife.

My mother's death was ruled a result of a pulmonary embolism, a major blockage of an artery in the lung. These can happen when a person has had long periods of inactivity or is suffering from a disease such as cancer. This was why Mom was having shortness of breath and eventually stopped breathing. The coroner stated that it was likely Mom was dead before being transported to the hospital.

"I can't believe she's gone. It's all my fault!" my father yells.

My Uncle John whispers a response. I'm not sure what he's saying. He has volunteered to spend the night with Dad, Kyle, and me. After returning from the hospital, the only visitors we have are my Uncle John and Aunt Cindy. Other people are most likely also in shock. Maybe they

29

believe that if they avoid the space of my mother's absence, they can avoid the reality of her death as well. Or perhaps they're trying to give us space.

Is the numbness I'm feeling denial or devastation? *I fucking hate you, God. How could you do this to us? To me?*

I continue focusing on the ceiling, trying not to think about what's ahead.

* * *

There's a country song about how everyone dies famous in a small town. My mother's death is definitely a testament to this. It's now the morning after her death, and family members, neighbors, friends, and even acquaintances have come flocking to our home. Some people bring food—from tuna casseroles to cheese and sausage trays to fruit cobblers to cookies and donuts. Being an emotional eater, I've already devoured four types of donuts. The sugar feels good and soothing. No matter what happens, food will not disappoint me. Then I remember that my mom is dead, and I feel my stomach cringe.

Some family members not only bring food but also offer housekeeping services. My Aunt Debbie has vacuumed the living room, dusted the coffee tables, and swept the kitchen floor—twice. "I like to keep busy when I'm anxious," she says.

My brother has been hiding in his bedroom all morning. Whereas I barely was able to sleep last night, sleeping is his way of coping. Even with his television droning on in the background, he's able to continue a deep slumber. I wish I could do the same and escape this harsh reality through dreaming.

Dad has maintained a solemn demeanor. He's been interacting with people all morning almost as if he's on autopilot. Step one: Answer the never-ending ringing phone and have a conversation. Step two: Chat with visitors while ignoring the never-ending ringing phone. Make statements like "I hate that she's gone, but she is no longer in pain." Step three: Pick at a piece of food. Step four: Go to Kyle's bedroom and make sure he's still breathing. Repeat steps one through four.

The family priest, Father Jerome, stops by our house. He had been with us the night before, in the hospital, to give Mom her last rites. At one point in the morning, Father Jerome and my Aunt Janet (who hasn't attended a church service in at least five years) sit across from one another in our living room. Jerome, known for being a staunch Catholic

GOODBYE

fundamentalist, allows my aunt's grief to excuse any potential lectures he may want to give about church attendance. That still doesn't prevent him from giving her a slightly reprimanding glare over his coffee mug.

Time escapes us, and the minutes slip into hours. All of my mother's siblings—her four sisters and two brothers—are gathered in the kitchen with me while my father chats with neighbors in the living room. Stories about Mom come in waves, and then there are moments of devastated silence. Why should we not talk about the happy moments we spent with the deceased? It's better than thinking about our future attempts to live without them.

"I keep thinking about how much pain she was in over the last few months," I say to Aunt Susie. She's the youngest of my mother's sisters, and many believe she looks the most like my mother.

"I know," Susie responds and pats my arm gently. "Just think about how happy she is now. She's in Heaven with Grandpa Corky, Aunt Betty, Uncle Jack . . . your Grandma and Grandpa Paxton."

I nod my head slowly. I try to envision my mother excitedly being greeted by the previous deceased relatives, but my attempts are interrupted. My mind turns to yesterday when I observed Randy giving her CPR. I did not tell Dad, but at one point I saw my mother's eyes widen in horror as she gasped for breath. Squeezing my eyes tightly and wincing in pain, I try to shake the ominous vision, but it keeps playing over and over.

"Yesterday," I stammer. "When . . . when she was lying there on the floor. She just kept struggling for breath and she looked *so scared.*"

And then the horrific visions overcome me and shatter the constant numbness I've been feeling since last night. I hear a sound rise out of my gut and into the air—one that feels foreign and nonhuman. Sobbing uncontrollably, I fall into Aunt Susie's arms. The familiarity of her embrace, just like my mother's, causes more tears to flow. But there's something comfortable about letting go of all control and making room for my grief.

The only problem is that I want to stay in Aunt Susie's arms forever and not face the hard reality of life without my mother.

* * *

My mother looks like she's sleeping.

This isn't my first encounter with death. I've been to funeral services for three grandparents, a great-aunt, and a great-uncle. I remember when I first

31

saw these deceased relatives I felt extreme fear. When I was eight and saw my Grandma Paxton's body, I ran and hid in the funeral home bathroom.

I'm not afraid now. I look at my mother in the casket, and I feel a mix of sadness and relief. Her hair is perfectly curled, and she's wearing her usual amount of makeup. The outfit her sisters picked—a floral dress with soft color mixes of red, violet, and blue—is definitely fitting. It matches her vibrant personality. I extend my hand and consider touching her, but then I retract. It is almost as if I'm in an awkward dance with death—trying to find the delicate balance between holding on and letting go.

I think back to my birth and wonder what the moment was like for her. After my delivery, when she rocked me in her arms, I'm sure the idea of leaving me at eighteen never crossed her mind. Moments of birth and moments of death—are these the ultimate moments of intimacy between a parent and a child?

My Aunt Debbie caresses the side of the casket. "She looks so pretty and at peace."

During many funeral preparation periods, it seems that the decision whether to have an open casket is often one of contention. However, with Mom there is nothing that visibly scarred her body. After seeing the hell that her disease unleashed upon it, I'm sure I'm not the only one who finds viewing the body therapeutic.

It seems as if the whole town has decided to come to Mom's visitation service. Father Jerome says out of his whole career in the priesthood this is the longest line he has ever seen. The line goes down the church steps and wraps around the sidewalk almost two miles down the street. Those who have come to pay their respects are a mixture of many different types of acquaintances: family friends and neighbors, clients of my mother's, my father's co-workers, and some of Kyle's and my schoolmates. There are people here I would never have expected to attend—some of the "cool dudes" at school who like to torment me.

Brent Wadley and his older brother John approach me in the visiting line. I recoil, because these are two brothers who have had received pleasure from pinning me against a wall, twisting my nipples, and calling me a faggot. *Why are they here?*

John places a sympathetic hand on my shoulder, with his eyes downcast. "I'm sorry, man. If you need anything at all, let us know."

Maybe you could stop being a jerk? I guess sometimes loss can't always bring people together, especially when past actions poison offers of sympathy.

I'm surprised that I haven't cried during the visitation. Instead, I'm one of the most cheerful members of my family. With a big toothy grin, I chat animatedly and optimistically with each person who comes to pay respects. It's as if I'm one of those windup dolls—someone keeps pulling my string and then off I go. It's surprising that I'm less emotional than most of Mom's visitors. Then again, I've been drowning in grief for the last forty-eight hours.

Most people offer the typical statements of condolence: "I'm sorry for your loss." "Your mamma is in a better place." "She is no longer in pain." "I know what you are going through." Or "I know how you feel." I nod politely and thank them, because this is what I'm supposed to do. Who wants to see a negative son at his mother's funeral? I do my best to compartmentalize my emotions, even though I'm broken inside.

The emotional reactions among the crowd are gendered. The men stand stoic and offer humorous stories from the past. The women, some of whom I never thought I would ever share such intimacy, can barely speak through sobs as they hug my brother and me tightly. Ms. Schwartz approaches me. She was one of Mom's clients, and right before her appointments we used to have to hide Maddie because Ms. Schwartz supposedly hated animals and children. Schwartz, in her fifties and never married, often would complain about the weather and some town residents' un-Christian like behaviors. "Do not come out here for the next hour," Mom used to warn us. "Her haircut and color might buy you guys another video game, so scat!" These sorts of warnings would often work. However, one time my brother accidentally walked in, observed Schwartz's color treatment, and exclaimed, "Geez! Your hair sure looks orange!" Schwartz did not appreciate this, and Mom was surprised that she returned to the salon after that.

Chuckling from this memory, I try to use it to distract myself from gagging, because Schwartz's embrace brings forth the pungent smell of mothballs. "You poor things!" she squeals. "At least you got your daddy. You all are gonna be strong for him, okay? Just find peace in knowing your mom is with Jesus!"

"Thank you for coming, Ms. Schwartz," I say, hoping that she'll release me from her taut, nauseating grip. She moves forward in the line, and I catch my brother watching and giggling at the latest spectacle. I shrug and give him a look that says, *Hey, I'm not the one who told her that her hair looked orange.*

I'm pleasantly surprised when I see four of my co-workers walking forward in line. We do like to have fun at work, but we rarely express or talk about our feelings. My breath catches when I see Brooke—one of the female servers in the restaurant.

Brooke is what some might call a "natural beauty," reminding me of actress Angelina Jolie. She's tall, with dark brown hair and eyes. Pink, luscious lips frame her bright, white smile. I don't know much about makeup, but I doubt she wears much, if any. Brooke's father and my father have been good friends, and she had sometimes accompanied her father on visits to our home. She and I would often talk about our mutual interests in journalism and speech communication. She works as a server to pay for college and fund her future career as a public relations specialist. At work, after small conversations with her in the middle of a lunch or dinner rush period, I'd often daydreamed about what it would be like to marry her and start a family. I would be so normal if that happened, and we would be happy. Wouldn't we?

The warm feelings from my reveries continue as she hugs and consoles me. "How are you doing?" she coos.

"As well as can be expected," I respond. I need to make sure I show masculine strength. *Don't be a wimp.*

"I know what you're going through."

Brooke's father died about five years ago from a brain tumor. "If you need anything, let me know."

I nod to thank her.

I continue to greet more people in the line—never taking a break. Before I know it, three hours have passed. I find myself feeling *happy*. My face hurts from smiling, and I feel guilty about this. *How could you smile at your mother's funeral?* I'm not happy she died, but I'm happy that so many people love us and have come to show their support.

The happy, supported feelings don't last for long. When we get home, I sense my mother's absence. I crawl into bed and softly weep into my pillows. Sleep doesn't come easily tonight.

* * *

We receive a foot of snow overnight. Dad has already been notified that some staff members have been to church and shoveled off the sidewalks. Two to three more inches are expected later in the day.

In the early morning hours on the day of my mother's burial, we're well on our way to receiving a foot of snow, and I'm struggling with insomnia. I get out of bed and sit alone in the living room, staring at my mother's curio cabinet full of snowman figurines and snow globes. Eventually I get up from the chair, reach into the cabinet, and begin to slowly handle each artifact. It might be mindless tinkering to help me cope with my anxiety, but I feel my mother's presence in every touch of her prized possessions.

Suddenly I feel a smile spread across my stiff and tear-soaked face. I look out the window toward the morning sky and say, "Looks like you got your big snow of the year. You never had trouble making your presence known."

* * *

The snow doesn't stop loved ones from paying their respects, and every pew in the church is full. We share stories about Mom and review pictures from various points in her life. Everyone laughs when we see Mom and Dad in old pictures from school dances. Mom is sporting a tight-knit '80s perm, and Dad is without a beard and has the same haircut John Travolta had in *Saturday Night Fever*. The beautiful memories encapsulated through photographs keep coming: an image of Mom cutting my hair in her salon when I was six, a moment in which she's posing with my brother in his uniform on the football field, and a picture with eight of her closest high school friends on a cruise liner—her last vacation.

A few family members participate in the service. My cousin gives a lovely eulogy filled with compassion and humor. My brother, a young man who usually utters few words, has written and read a poem. And I decide to sing for her.

I stand in the church rafters and look down at the full rows of pews. My brother and father, along with my grandmother and my aunts and uncles, are in the first three rows. Some are staring ahead in the distance—still in shock. Others cry and cuddle in one another's embrace. My father places his arm behind my brother's back, slightly massaging his neck.

Taking a few deep breaths, I approach the music stand. I glance at the organ player and give him my nod of approval. I am ready. I can do this. I *want* to do this. My mother supported me in my academic and artistic pursuits, and I believe this is one final way I can honor her. Many of my family members have reassured me over the last couple of days that if I should break down while singing it'll be okay. Others have cautioned against me singing at the funeral.

But I'm determined, though nervous.

Originally, I wanted to pick a song that my mother enjoyed or one that represented the many loving relationships that she had with other people. However, this service is in a Catholic church, and Father Jerome was adamant that I choose a religious hymn. We decided that I would sing the Lord's Prayer.

Upon hearing the organ, my heartbeat quickens. I follow my voice instructor's advice and make sure to take slow, deep breaths. It's hard to breathe normally because I can see my mother's body in the casket. *God. This is really it.* Fighting back tears, I begin the first line.

Our father, which art in heaven. Hallowed be thy name.

I try to focus on happy moments with Mom. My mind goes to the many times she watched me sing in the past. I reflect on my first solo. In the third grade, my music teacher led a program in which the theme was "Music Around the World." My class represented Mexico, and I adorned the stereotypical outfit of sandals, a sombrero, and a bullfighter cape. The finale of the program consisted of me and three other peers singing lines from Lee Greenwood's "God Bless the USA." Mom took me out for ice cream afterward.

I remember the excitement of future possibilities for her child gleaming in her eyes. She had said, "My sweet boy. You have such a beautiful voice!"

My response was a big cheesy smile smeared with ice cream, my sombrero slipping off and cocked to the side of my head.

Thy kingdom come. Thy will be done. On Earth as it is in Heaven.

My memory turns to my eighth-grade graduation ceremony. Many in our community had joked that I won so many school awards that I would need a dump truck to help my parents take them home. I also sang lines from Lee Ann Womack's "I Hope You Dance." In the weeks leading up to the ceremony, Mom would play the song in the car and help me practice. The threat of tears becomes more intense when I think about how she won't be able to attend my high school graduation.

Give us this day our daily bread. And forgive us our debts as we forgive our debtors. And lead us not into temptation but deliver us from evil.

"Blakey! Blake, come sing for us!"

This was a phrase that Mom would often yell from her salon. There were several elderly ladies who got their hair styled every week—the "weeklies," as we called them. Every chance she had, my mother would ask me to perform for them. I remember several of the gray-haired ladies gleefully clapping and praising me. "That boy is going to be famous one day!" they would say. "Ann, he truly has a special gift!"

For thine is the kingdom.

I'm building intensity. I need to breathe.

And the power.

Breathe, Blake. Breathe.

And the glory. For—

Here comes the big moment—the part of the song with the highest vocal range.

EEEVERRR...

Warmth tingles throughout my body. Maybe it's God. Maybe it's my mother's love. But it soothes me in my grief. I look at the crowd and see two of my aunts crying.

Amen.

* * *

Snow continues to fall softly during the burial. I watch the flakes collect on the top of my mother's casket. The overcast gray sky and the cool wind seem to reflect everyone's mood: a quiet devastation. Most people knew my mother was in much pain during her illness, and, as in most small towns, I'm sure there were many discussions about her progress.

Progress.

We were always asking, "What's next? Which surgery? Which treatment?" My mother's community of grievers fell into the trap of commonly accepted ideas of illness—that this rare disease was something to be fought and defeated. With little information, we were all unaware about the possibility of her illness being terminal. Palliative care or hospice never entered discussions surrounding my mother's condition. Why would they? To many people, my mother seemed too young to die—too *important* to die.

Now, the lips of the townspeople no longer move as they watch my mother being lowered into the ground.

* * *

After all the services have been completed, my Aunt Cindy and Uncle John join my father, Kyle, and me back at home. My aunt nervously sweeps the nearly spotless kitchen floor. She also puts away some folded laundry as my uncle chats with us in the living room.

"Are you guys hungry?" she asks. "I can fix some hamburgers."

"Oh, no!" my father quickly interjects. "We're fine. Right, guys?"

Kyle and I nod. I barely ate at the funeral luncheon, and despite the growling I feel in my stomach, I don't wish to eat. It has been hard to distinguish between hunger and nausea lately.

"All right, then. I guess we'll leave, John. You sure you guys don't need anything?" Cindy inquires as she gives each of us a tight hug.

"No, no. We'll let you know if we need any help," my father reassures her.

After they both leave, we sit silently in the living room. My father listlessly flips through channels on the television. Maddie is lying on the couch, staring into the distance—the glare of the flashing television illuminates her exasperated expression. Dogs sense things, too.

"She's really gone, guys," Dad chokes out. "But we'll be okay."

In this moment of emptiness, it finally sinks in that Mom is gone. *What do we do now?* I think as we sit in silence. *What do we do now that the ritual, the show, of death is over, and we're left with the hard reality of loss?*

* * *

I catch my father in a private moment of grief.

It's about two months after Mom's funeral. He has left the door open to the bedroom he shared with Mom. Sitting at the foot of their bed, he grasps the answering machine in his hands. He has a blank expression. He stares off and presses the play button for the second time. My mother's voice fills the room:

> "Hi, Lindon! Hi, Blake! Hi, Kyle! Hi, Maddie! It's so beautiful here! I just wanted to call and let you know I'm doing great and having a blast. I love you and I will see you soon!"

She left the message while she was on a cruise to the Bahamas with her high school friends. My father has played this message every day since she died. In a strange way, it seems as if she's directly speaking to us from Heaven. I think this is why the message comforts Dad. Maybe he also just wants to hear her voice.

He hits the play button again.

"Hi, Lindon, Hi—"

Suddenly my mother's voice is silenced by an automated voice message.

"Message deleted."

Dad's mouth drops open in horror. "What?" he mutters and begins to frantically push buttons on the machine.

"No new messages."

He begins to pound the answering machine against the wooden bed frame. "Piece of fucking shit!" Every slam gains speed, intensity, and more cursing.

My breath catches as he leaps from the bed. He lets out a roar comparable to a wild animal. As he yells, he lifts the machine over his head, yanking the plug out the outlet, and throws it against the wall. He then falls to his knees and sobs into the mattress.

I move into the bedroom and embrace him.

In this moment, I feel this hardened man crumble. This is the same man who worked twelve-hour shifts in a coal mine for eighteen years. This is the same man who would tell me to tough it out whenever one of the neighborhood kids would give me a bloody nose. This is the same man who believes in the value of hard work and preventing emotional displays.

This same man's grief allows him to seek comfort in his eldest son's arms. But instead of feeling my body become soft, I sense resistance. In a time when we should be able to grieve together, I feel empty—numb. His tears fall onto my cold, hard body.

I try to fight the numbness and sympathize as much as I can. "I know this is hard for you. You were going to have to get rid of that message at some point," I say.

"I know," he murmurs. "I just can't believe she's gone."

He takes my face in his hands. I watch his bloodshot eyes search mine. Maybe he senses my emotional resistance and is searching for compassion, trying to understand why his son is defiant.

"Every time I look at you boys, I see your mom. I know you can't help it, but it hurts me sometimes to even look at you," he says. I continue to hug him in silence.

Chapter 2

RE-MEMBERING

My mother is crying.

She sheds tears of joy as she sits in front of the television set.

I am about thirteen years old and at the developmental stage that Piaget would call "formal operational." My childhood obsessions with magic, witches, curses, and spells have lapsed.

Feeling slightly troubled, I hesitate in sharing my mother's enthusiasm for the television show she's watching. It seems to be placing a spell of emotional reverie upon her. She sits clutching her hand to her chest. Her eyes are glazed over and misty.

My mother's watching "Crossing Over With John Edward." Edward is a popular psychic medium from New York. Gathering large audiences together in his studio every week, he supposedly passes on messages from the dead. Once he has honed in on a family in the audience, he starts asking them questions. He makes statements like "Someone is coming through with an M name. It's a female. Maria? Marla? Marissa?"

There's usually an excited recognition among the family members. Edward proceeds to tell them information that only those close to the family would know. Sometimes he can guess the name of the family dog. Or he knows a favorite meal of the deceased family member who is "coming through."

It's almost as if Edward is Jesus Christ to his audience members, but I believe he's a fraud. I consider my mother one of his innocent victims.

"It's fake, Mom."

As the ending credits float on the screen, my mother quickly shuts off the television. She turns to me in exasperation. "No it isn't! How could he have known that information?"

I cringe defensively and squirm in my chair. Mom and I are close, so when there's any disagreement between us I feel uncomfortable. "He probably has snoops get information about audience members before the show," I reply, but I can't get myself to meet her gaze. My right index finger anxiously strokes the dog-eared pages of a paperback novel as I await her response.

"Do you not remember what happened with Grandpa Corky and the keys?"

I raise an eyebrow and shake my head slowly back and forth.

"Ha!" My mother's face shines with excitement and she jabs her finger at me from across the room. "You want proof? Here's a story that will impress you!"

Aside from being a highly respected hairdresser in our small town, my mother has taken on the role of master storyteller and counselor for her clients. She's known not only for providing a great service to her patrons but also for her many entertaining talents.

"What story, Mom?" I ask begrudgingly.

"Your grandfather used to have a set of keys to his vending machine business. Even after he retired, he carried those keys around as a good luck charm. When the cancer was at its worst, you remember your grandfather was not very right in his mind. He would constantly yell about his missing keys. No one in our family could ever find them. We eventually forgot about them, and then he went into the hospital. A day after he died, the family was gathered at his home. Your cousin Seth leaned back in his old recliner and bam! His keys fell out!"

I roll my eyes.

Ignoring my skepticism, she continues. "He sat in that chair all the time, but the keys just happened to fall out the day after he died. He was telling us that he's around and okay!"

"All right, Mom." My tone is slightly condescending.

My mother sighs. "I am very proud of you, but sometimes I think you are too smart for your own good. There are ways in which we can connect with those who have died. You'll understand one day."

"Welcome to 7M!" Stephanie, my resident advisor, proclaims, smiling from ear to ear.

I snap out of my memories. *Get it together, Blake. Now is not the time to be sentimental.*

It's the night before first-year orientation begins. It took me a while to believe that I would go to college after Mom's death. After graduating high school, I had considered taking a year off and helping Dad at home. "No way," he said whenever I suggested this. "Your mom would not have wanted that."

And so, after looking at a few schools, I choose a school in St. Louis. Dad and I joked that Mom and Grandpa were trying to give me a sign that this was the school for me when we realized one of the university's main streets shared my grandfather's first name. Also, during a campus tour of the student recreation center, a special on hairdressers came on several of the center's televisions.

This university also has the kind of degree program I want. In addition, the campus is laid out in a way that many students claim it feels as if you're living in a small community. This is perfect for me, because I'm able to explore the city lifestyle I've craved but at the same time feel comfortable in a culture similar to that of my hometown.

Stephanie has gathered all the students on my floor in the common lounge area to help us get to know one another and go over this week's schedule of events. I'm excited but also overwhelmed because the organizers seem to have every minute of each day scheduled. I'm looking forward to the Country Western–themed dance party at the end of the week.

I look around at the forty-eight faces, both male and female, of the students who will be my neighbors (and hopefully friends) for the next year. *I hope there aren't any jerks.*

Continuing to beam, Stephanie pulls out a few plastic grocery bags. She dumps their contents on the floor. They contain art supplies—a myriad of colored pencils, glue sticks, and scissors. "We're going to be artists tonight!"

There's a mixed chorus of uttered responses. Some students groan and roll their eyes. Others smile and give cheers of joy. I am indifferent. I want to get to know everybody, but I'm not much of a visual artist.

Stephanie continues to give the group directions. We all have to draw a coat of arms. The theme for our floor is Medieval Life. Well, I did think the knight in shining armor door decorations were cool. After everyone completes their coat of arms, we have to spend a few moments sharing them with the group. Most of the students speak animatedly about their hometowns and families. As I hear each presentation, my heartbeat quickens. I don't often get nervous about giving presentations, but there's something about this one that rattles me.

I get through my presentation. For something I had so much anxiety about, it seemed to go quickly. I look back at the forty-eight pairs of eyes, attempting to gauge their thoughts. *Do they know what was missing from my coat of arms? And if any of them does, am I going to get asked about it?*

No one asks about the missing person in the description of my family.

* * *

I slowly pull a wooden block from the Jenga stack, and I'm relieved when the stack doesn't topple. *I'm still in the game.* This game of Jenga is different than the one I'm used to. My floor mates have constructed "Dare Jenga." On the back of some of the blocks are dare statements they've written. In order to stay in the game, you have to complete the dare should your block have one.

Turning over my block, I brace myself for what it might say. I feel sick when I see a dare that reads, "Kiss a person of the group's choosing." I've never *really* kissed anyone. This is something I have much shame and have told only a handful of people about.

After reading the dare out loud, I hear a chorus of mischievous squeals and giggles. *All right, let's get this over with.* I watch a few of my friends whisper and debate my kissing prospects. After a brief minute, my friend Paige proudly proclaims, "We want you to kiss . . . Denton!"

The hairs on the back of my neck stand on end. *Oh shit! Denton.* This is the guy on our floor whose sexuality is frequently questioned. He acts interested in men and women but never explicitly states how he identifies.

I've had a crush on him since move-in day. I had to move in early before everyone else because I got a job as a security-desk worker for the residence hall. I loved working the first shift during move-in because I got to greet the incoming students. Denton had been kind enough to bring me a soda. The infatuation started then.

And now I've been dared to kiss him.

I look over at Denton to see his reaction. He's leaning back in his chair, arms crossed, with a cool and collected smile.

My body begins to move toward him. *Yes, I'm moving. This is really happening.* Our faces come within inches of each other, and heat radiates between us. Our lips touch and we have a brief and awkward kiss. *That's it? This is what all the fuss is about?*

While the kiss is not phenomenal, the event is significant.

I finally feel like I know who I am.

Later in the evening, Mom meets me in my dreams. I wake up startled, with beads of sweat rolling down my face. *Would she have approved of this kiss?*

I have trouble going back to sleep. I tell myself to forget about the kiss and that all will be better in the morning.

***

"Dad, I got a summer job!"

My first year in college has flown by quickly. It's the last day of final exams week, and I feel so relieved. I'm sure I got all A's this semester. I let my father know this as well, and he's pleased.

He asks, "So are they going to let you go back to work at Alongi's?"

I nervously look down at my desk and doodle in my notebook. "Um . . . no. I got a job on campus."

I'm not sure what to make of the silence. Is he disappointed?

Finally he responds: "The dorms are open over the summer? How are you going to pay for housing?"

"Yes, the dorms are open. I will be working as an office assistant for our student housing office. If you work for any of the university offices, your housing is paid for in the summer."

"Ah. That's a good deal. Are your friends around?"

When I had asked my friends whether they planned to stay on campus over the summer, many of them looked at me with bewilderment. *Why would we do that?* Their expressions seemed to say.

"Yeah, a few," I respond.

I love living in a city. There is always something to do—even if it's something as simple as enjoying an espresso at the local Starbucks. The nearest Starbucks to my hometown is 45 minutes away and has limited hours. Plus, I can be *me* here, embracing the warm summer nights and joining the flocks at the local gay clubs.

I snap out of my reveries of flashing lights, pulsating beats, and hard bodies. I need to give my father a rationale for my decision, but it's difficult to think of a reason because I haven't yet told him I'm gay.

I decide to tell a trivial lie. "I hear that the more time you invest in the housing office, the better chances you have of getting a resident advisor position. If I'm a resident advisor, my housing is paid for all year."

This seems to satisfy him. "Okay. That's fine. I'm proud of you, son."

"Thanks, Dad."

"It's good that you are only 90 minutes away. You can come home on the weekends."

"Sure." But as I utter the word, my mind drifts again to more reveries of male exotic dancers, drag queens, and dance floors.

* * *

"Why do you never talk about your family?"

He slowly massages my sweaty chest hair and lightly kisses my temple.

I tense under his warm and gentle embrace. "Why would I want to talk about my family after we've just hooked up?"

I realize the sharpness of my tone when I gaze into his eyes. It's too late. I've already hurt him.

"I just . . ." He turns away from me.

"You just what?" I push myself up from bed and against the headboard.

"I just feel like there's always a wall with you." He's out of bed now and pulling on his pants.

"What are you talking about? I told you I was tired before you came over tonight."

Fully clothed, he heads to the bedroom door.

"Wait!" I call out, and he turns to face me.

"Before you say anything," he begins, "I want you to know that I care about you. But lately all you want to do is have me come over . . . and that's fun, but I want you to take us seriously!"

"There never was an 'us.' *This*," I gesture from him to the bed, "was all we were supposed to have. What don't you get?"

He opens his mouth and then tightly purses his lips. His eyes glisten with tears.

"I hate you," he whispers. "Don't contact me again."

He storms out of my room and slams the door—the cool silence reminds me that he isn't the only person I've been pushing away.

* * *

I haven't spoken to my brother in months. It's the second week of November, and Thanksgiving is quickly approaching.

Our silence is broken when he calls on a Wednesday evening.

"Hello, stranger." His tone is playful.

"Hi, Kyle."

"I was wondering if your hand was broken."

"Why?"

"I hadn't heard from you in a while."

"I'm sorry. School has been crazy."

"It's okay. Are you coming home for Thanksgiving?"

"Yes."

The rest of the conversation is devoted to finalizing the details of my visit. It's easier to bypass talking about feelings when you have travel itineraries to discuss.

* * *

The day has finally come for my undergraduate graduation ceremony. The four years passed quickly, and I've shed many tears and given goodbye hugs to my friends. A few of them have been offered jobs that will take them to other parts of the country—even other parts of the world. I've been accepted into a graduate program in communication at the University of South Florida (USF) in Tampa. My studies will be fully funded through a teaching assistantship, and I'm excited about the move. I try not to think about the summer I'll have to spend at home before I leave for USF. I won't be able to work on campus and receive free housing this summer, because I'll no longer be a student.

This is a Catholic school, and the graduation ceremony takes place in the campus church, where every Sunday night priests held mass for the students. Dad jokingly said they held it on Sunday nights to give the students enough time to recover from their hangovers. I found that the priests did an exceptional job of relating to students, giving homilies on contemporary and pertinent issues. A student choir and full band provided music at every service. It was the only Catholic service that I had been to where, aside from standing and kneeling, people clapped and danced in the pews. The services here and the church community helped restore my faith in God, so that two years ago I made my family proud by deciding to become a confirmed Catholic.

In my high school graduation ceremony, I was given a singing solo. I remember how everyone praised my rendition of Whitney Houston's "One Moment in Time." But when my mother died, my love of singing publicly did as well. During college, instead of to music I devoted my time to student political groups and research endeavors. So in today's ceremony, I have no performance.

I look out from the rows of graduating students and find my father and stepmother's beaming faces. Kelly, my stepmother, has been great for my father. Growing up, because I didn't know many kids who had stepparents, the only representations I had of stepmothers were the wicked ones from the movies. However, I've never considered Kelly wicked, and I like her a lot. She knew my mother and had gone to her a few times for haircuts.

Kelly and my father found love in the local grocery store, a couple of years after Mom died. One day my father ran into Kelly in the produce aisle, and, knowing that her father had died recently, offered his condolences. The two of them got to talking, but she turned down his invitation for a date. After two more attempts, Kelly finally accepted. This led to several more dates, Kelly moving into my childhood home, and their marriage a year and a half later. My father seems much happier with her in his life, and although the blended family (she has four adult children) has resulted in some conflict, we continue to work through the challenges.

The baccalaureate graduation ceremony is pleasant. The church is more than 100 years old and, like most Catholic churches, has beautiful stained-glass windows. A few student representatives give short speeches on our hopefully bright futures. The choir sings a few hymns, and some scripture is read. At last, the president of the university—a short, stout, balding priest—gives his concluding address. The speech is religious but general enough for students of many faiths and backgrounds. He ends by stating that we'll be sons and daughters of the university forever and that we can make a difference in this broken world. By this point, I've glanced at my watch four times and am ready to leave. The band starts playing exit music, and, as the choir sings, students slowly shuffle row by row out the church doors.

I find my parents outside, at the bottom of the front steps. Dad reaches out, grabs me by the shoulder, and pulls me in for a hug. "Hey, man! That was a nice ceremony! You ready for tomorrow?"

"Hell yeah," I respond.

My stepmother, Kelly, looks at the two of us admiringly. "You have a lot to be proud of, Blake. Think about where you want to eat tomorrow after commencement. It'll be our treat."

My stomach growls in anticipation as I think about going to one of my favorite restaurants that serves giant cheeseburgers, greasy French fries, and root beer floats.

Dad's bright expression dims somewhat. "Your mom is proud of you too."

"I know . . . I know," I say quickly.

Unexpectedly, my father asks, "Did you feel that little ray of sunshine on you earlier?"

"What?"

"I was thinking about your mom, and all of a sudden a ray of sunshine came through the stained-glass windows, and it was only shining on you and nobody else."

I slightly pull away from his embrace. "Oh, come on, Dad . . ."

He turns to my stepmother in exasperation. "I'm not kidding. Kelly, you saw it too! Tell him!"

Kelly nods.

In order to not ruin these joyful moments, I accept the possibility that a ray of sunlight could be communication from Mom. "That's neat, Dad," I say, mustering some enthusiasm.

I continue to possess many masks and have become a pro at covering— covering my sexual orientation, covering my anger at God, covering my grief. But no matter how much I try, I sense they can sense my skepticism about Dad's hopeful observation.

* * *

We only have an hour left in the drive to Tampa.

I notice the differences in terrain once we pass the Florida state line. Many vacationing tourists might believe their trips to Tampa or Miami or Disney World in Orlando are almost finished once they reach the state line. However, they soon realize that the state is much larger than they thought.

I can barely contain my sense of urgency. I try to focus on a novel, but I read one or two sentences and then look back out the window. My knee begins to shake—even though it's been hours since I've had any caffeine.

My father looks back from the driver's seat. "Everything okay back there?"

"Yes," I respond. "Just excited."

"Only three more hours!" Kelly exclaims from the passenger seat.

I smile as I look at the palm trees. It was about nine years ago that I was sitting in the family car on the same route to Tampa.

"We are going on this vacation without any whiny men!" Mom had said.

I was thirteen years old when my mother decided to take a family vacation to Florida. She asked one of her best friends, Kate, to go with us. Kate often discussed how her husband didn't like to travel. My father also was not much of a traveler. So, Mom, Kate, my brother, and I packed up and decided to head to Tampa to visit some family members, spend time on the beach, and go to an amusement park.

Many pleasant memories came from this trip. We were able to see an aunt and a cousin who we hadn't seen in years. I got to challenge my fears and scream ferociously on skyscraper-high roller coasters. I got to embrace the warm sunshine, collect seashells, and revel in the cool ocean water between my toes as I walked along the tide.

It was definitely a memorable trip. This was before I came out as gay. I chuckle when I think about a moment when my mom believed her sexuality was being questioned. We had all decided to stop at a small diner on the way home from our vacation. Mom and Kate were both dressed comfortably for the long drive home. Mom, who was usually pretty adamant about wearing makeup, decided to forgo her normal beauty regimen that day. I can't remember everything the server said to Mom and Kate, but I do remember when she brought the check she handed it to Mom and said, "Whenever you're ready."

Shortly after, I can remember Kate's high-pitched giggling as we walked through the parking lot. "She thought we were lesbians, Kate! And I was the butch one in the relationship!" Mom then quickly walked behind Kate and gave her butt an exaggerated pinch. "Hey, baby!" Kate doubled over with laughter. This playful banter continued until we reached the car.

Mom had joked about the server's assumptions. She hadn't acted offended or commented on the morality of same-sex relationships. This gives me some glimmer of hope that she would have been supportive of me.

"We're here!" Kelly exclaims. "Look how nice your apartment building is!"

I look ahead at what will be my next home and feel optimistic about the next part of my journey.

* * *

The sand feels pleasantly warm between my fingers and toes. I stare off into the distance—watching people frolic through the ocean waves.

This is Florida.

Pass-a-Grille Beach in St. Petersburg, Florida.

Tampa, Florida, is my new home.

My friends in Illinois joke that I've become a hippie beach bum, running away never to return again.

"Does the anniversary of her death ever get easier for you?" My friend Tasha looks up at me while lounging on her towel. Today is the anniversary of her mother Dede's death. Dede died when she was forty-five years old, from septicemia. I consider Tasha one of my best friends, and our common experience of suffering the loss of a parent at a young age has strengthened our bond.

I take a sip from my vodka cranberry. "I always think it'll get easier, but it seems like it gets more difficult. Another year has gone by full of things that she has not been able to be a part of . . . You know what I mean?"

Tasha sighs wistfully. "Yes."

Our reflections on life, death, and mothers are interrupted when we hear "Mom! I want to swim! Let me go . . . please?!"

We watch a boy of about six attempting to escape his mother's loving hold. They move as if in an awkward dance. The mother has a bottle of sunblock in one hand and is grasping her son's arm in the other. He flails in resistance.

"Hey, buddy," I say.

The boy stops flailing. His eyes widen.

"Hi," he responds. His mother gives me a suspicious look. I usually don't involve myself in parental woes, but for some reason I feel compelled to do so today.

I point to my shoulders. "I don't know if you can see . . . but do you see all these freckles?"

"Yes."

"When I was a little older than you, I decided to not wear sunscreen. Those freckles used to be huge blisters, and they *hurt*. I was in pain for a long time. You'll get to swim, but let your mamma put some sunscreen on you."

The boy shakes his head rapidly up and down. "Okay. Mom, put it on! Put it on!"

His mother smiles at me.

Tasha giggles. "Nice work, BB." (She calls me BB and I call her TT. I'm not quite sure of the origin of these nicknames.)

"Just to be clear," I explain to her, "my mother was at work, and the babysitter did not put sunscreen on me. You can't blame the girl, though. It was an unseasonably warm day in March. All the neighborhood kids decided to play with water balloons, my shirt came off, and then you can probably figure out the rest. . ."

"Already the exhibitionist at such a young age," Tasha jokes.

"Ha! Yeah."

We fall silent. It's a weekday, so the beach isn't very crowded. Mostly we hear waves crashing and the chorus of seagulls. I imagine Tasha reflecting on a moment of motherly care from her youth. I lean over and give her a side hug.

"It must get easier to cope with their deaths," I say. "We'll figure something out."

* * *

The missing link has to be here somewhere.

In the middle of my bedroom floor, I'm drowning in a sea of books and articles. I've reviewed articles on many topics this afternoon: basic models of bereavement, children grieving the loss of a parent, friendship and social support after a loved one's death, the role of shared reminiscing among the bereaved, the benefits of bereavement support groups for those who share a similar loss. The pages of the books are festooned with multicolored tabs. Some of the books are half opened and face down. Others are in stacks that threaten to crumble into one messy heap. I pick up an article titled "The Incidence and Course of Depression in Bereaved Youth 21 Months After the Loss of a Parent to Suicide, Accident, or Sudden Natural Death" (Brent, Melhem, Donohoe, & Walker, 2009). *There might be something here*, I think. I read the results section in the abstract:

> Bereavement and a past history of depression increased depression risk in the 9 months following the death, which increased depression risk between 9 and 21 months. Losing a mother, blaming others, low self-esteem, negative coping, and complicated grief were associated with depression in the second year.
>
> (p. 786)

A chill goes up the back of my neck as I underline in red pen the phrase "losing a mother." I guess I'm lucky I never became addicted to alcohol or drugs.

Another article beckons from a nearby stack. "Time Does Not Heal All Wounds: Mortality Following the Death of a Parent" (Rostila & Saarela, 2011). *Lovely. How death leads to even more death.* I highlight a line that reads, "A mother's death tended to have a stronger influence than a father's death, unnatural parental deaths had a stronger effect than natural ones, and male offspring were more vulnerable than female offspring" (p. 236). I am glad that I have never considered ending my life.

Go to Carolyn's book chapter, a voice commands. Carolyn Ellis is my dear mentor and friend.

I must be losing it. Often, I joke with my students about hearing voices whenever a few are being rude while I'm trying to teach class. Some may find this method of reprimanding passive-aggressive, but it usually works. Ignoring my doubts about my own sanity, I pick up Carolyn's book chapter, "Seeking My Brother's Voice: Holding onto Long-Term Grief Through Photographs, Stories, and Reflections" (Ellis, 2013). It's an autoethnography in which Carolyn revisits an earlier article (Ellis, 1993) about the death of her younger brother Rex, who died in a plane crash on the way to visiting her. In this most recent work, she tries to figure out what it means to grieve the loss more than thirty years after it occurred.

I'd been a fan of Carolyn's even before I ever read this chapter. To me, she was the voice of autoethnography. I read every piece of her work I could access. The piece that spoke to me the most was "There Are Survivors: Telling a Story of Sudden Death" (Ellis, 1993). I felt the warm embrace of narrative resonance when I first read the opening line: "I grew up in a small town of three thousand people located in the foothills of Virginia, that same place my parents were born and raised" (p. 711). I no longer felt alone in my experience of sudden death, and through the experiencing of her experience (Ellis & Bochner, 1992), I came to appreciate my relationship with my younger brother.

Carolyn did not shy away from recounting the harsh details of the plane crash and her corresponding grief. I imagined myself in her position, in a situation that could have happened to me. My younger brother has visited me in Tampa. I would be devastated if he had died in a crash. Maybe I would feel some guilt—that there might've been something I could've done to prevent him from getting on the plane. As I read Carolyn's story for the first time, I remember cringing and yearning for hope that Rex would be okay. Carolyn described watching people being rescued from the water where the plane went down. I too felt compelled to scream with her, "Rex, emerge from the fucking water!"

Like me, Carolyn had experienced the sharp, gouging pain of the sudden death of a family member. Like me, she had observed the many different ways her family members grieved, while feeling as though she had to take care of everyone. Through our common experiences of death and grief, I came to realize the power of autoethnography.

Now I read her reflection chapter again (Ellis, 2013). Several quotes catch my attention:

> Stories about long-term grief are rare. My hope is that this story shows how grief can change over time and that it opens a conversation about the different ways the process of grieving might be experienced over a lifetime.
>
> (Ellis, 2013, p. 4)

There are many times I've felt disappointment when my mother couldn't be a part of major events in my life: my high school and college graduations, confirmation at church, research presentations. But I don't usually cry. *Does that mean I'm not still grieving?* I wonder. I think Carolyn makes a good point that there aren't enough studies on long-term grief. Maybe because the idea of long-term grief is threatening—threatening to the tough prototype many Americans are taught they must embody in times of sorrow. We all need to pick ourselves up by the bootstraps and move on. Right?

Carolyn continues:

> I suggest for many it can be healthy to hold on to grief as a way to maintain a relationship with a person who has died. Why should it be necessary to demand that those coping with the loss of a loved one's physical presence also detach from their feelings of love and need for the deceased?
>
> (p. 5)

I'm struck by the comment about it being healthy to hold on to grief. *Isn't this kind of like telling someone it's okay to continue pressing your hand on the top of a hot stove? Even if you did tell someone it was okay to hold on to grief, would the person know what you meant?* Then, I think about times when I've watched a movie or read a novel with an emotional ending and how crying, at such times, could be compared to savoring pieces of dark chocolate. *There's often a feeling of catharsis in those moments, and there's the concept of having a good cry—but are these moments different somehow? Less threatening?* Questions swirl in the air like a menacing fog. I read on:

> The complex emotions attached to my brother become part of my self and deepen my experience of living. The stories I tell keep him alive in my

memory. When others read my stories, my brother becomes someone readers and I have in common—he becomes a part of what they and I share. Thus, I do not experience my grief as pathological or unresolved, or something I desire to get rid of.

(p. 5)

I underline "The stories I tell keep him alive in my memory." This statement confirms my belief in communication as a process of social construction. We often think of communication happening *in* relationships, but a social constructionist view suggests that relationships happen *in* communication. A relationship with a deceased family member is at the center of a discursive struggle: discourses from psychiatry, religion, individual family, and community all conflict, pressuring an individual to choose between connecting and not connecting with the dead. And as I finish Carolyn's chapter, this discursive struggle becomes more apparent as she recounts some family members encouraging her to "re-member" Rex while others resist it.

When I finish reading, I sit in silence. *There is definitely something here, the missing link, but what is it?*

Then it hits me.

I excitedly clutch the chapter to my chest. *That's it!* I found the missing link to Tasha and my experiences. We are both helping each other continue relationships with and "re-member" our deceased mothers. Just as Carolyn tells stories about her brother to keep his memory alive, Tasha and I tell stories to each other to keep our memories of our mothers alive. Neither Tasha nor I ever met the other's mother, so when we tell stories about them it's an active and challenging process of reconstructing their presence. I can't wait to call Tasha and share what I've discovered.

Before I do that, however, there's something that I must do.

I pull out an old shoebox from underneath my bed. The box is brown and tattered, with bits flaking off at the corners. The power of its contents radiate on my fingertips. My hands shake . . . from what? Anxiety? Fear? Excitement? Maybe I feel all of these emotions. Joy, like the joy I feel every Christmas morning, surges through me when I pull off the top, but I already know what gifts are inside. Carefully, I place each of the box's treasures on the bed. They're all pictures that include my mother. There's one from our last family vacation together in Tampa in which she's laughing, dancing on the beach with a sassy finger pointed at the photographer. Then there's one of her in a glowing pink floral dress slow dancing with an elderly gentleman. I turn it over and in handwriting it says, "February 14, 2003, Amanda's wedding." Amanda is a cousin on my father's side of the family. Then there's a picture of my mother, my father, Grandpa Lindell, my brother, and me. Kyle looks about six or seven, and that would make me around ten or eleven. Grandpa looks thin, so this must have been in the final year of his illness from esophageal cancer. We're wearing dressy clothes and posing in front of some sort of bulletin board. I assume this is a church event. Then there are two photos with just Mom and me. One's from my junior prom, and she's helping me fix the tie on my tuxedo. The other's a picture of us in front of the Fabulous Fox Theater in St. Louis, Missouri.

This photo represents one of my fondest memories of spending time with Mom. She knew of my great love for the theater. After months of my pestering her, she surprised me with tickets to a performance of *West Side Story* for my twelfth birthday. It was the first time either of us had ever been to the theater, and it was a rare and extravagant event for two people from a small town. I got as much joy from watching my mother enjoy the performances as I did from the show itself. The faint hint of the song of the star-crossed lovers, Tony and Maria, fills my bedroom: "Tonight . . . tonight. . ."

This memory brings a smile to my face, and a tear rolls down my cheek. I reach up and touch it. Instead of wiping it away, I let my fingers feel the dampness of grief I've denied for so long. And in this moment, I also feel Mom's resurrection—not bringing her back to physical life but a resurrection of her presence in memory. I also feel resurrected from a deep and long neglect of our relationship.

* * *

"Whenever you hear me pause and say several 'Okays,' this is my way of validating the spirits I am hearing."

I never thought I would pay to receive a reading from a psychic medium. But after the insistence of several friends, I've decided to spend my Saturday afternoon at a boutique in St. Petersburg.

The psychic, Marguerite, is not what I expected. I'm used to the stereotypical representations of psychics in movies: women with brightly colored headscarves, gold hoop earrings and bracelets, flashy gowns, and a glowing crystal ball. Marguerite, on the other hand, looks about forty-five—and in jeans, sandals, and a light green T-shirt, she appears rather casual for a session of potential connections with the dead. Her office is located in a former home along the water in St. Pete Beach. The cost is $125 (cash only) for a reading that can last anywhere from forty-five to ninety minutes. When I scheduled the appointment over the phone, I was only asked to give my first name and a telephone number. I'm hoping this will be worth the time and money and that Marguerite is not a fraud. My academic side motivates me to have great skepticism.

I sit at Marguerite's kitchen table, tightly grasping a cup of coffee. The cup warms my cool, shaking hands. Marguerite explains how the session will work. "There might be people that you expect to come through. They may or may not decide to be here. You may be surprised at some of the spirits who visit. The spirits guide the session. They show me things and allow me to feel things, and I will respond to them with an 'Okay.' I request that you let them guide the questions, and they may have me ask you about several things, such as significant numbers or upcoming or past events. Over the years, spirits have shown me various common images that represent certain ideas. For instance, when they show me the snapping of fingers this means the person died quickly."

I nod my head to signal that I understand.

She continues, "I will be receiving all of this information, and together we can try to interpret what they are trying to say. If something doesn't make sense, I tell clients to write it down in the 'revisiting column.' Often, a detail may not make sense during a reading, but when clients go back to it later they remember something about the deceased that allows that detail to make sense. Do you have any questions before we begin?"

"No."

Marguerite sits upright in her chair, places both hands on the table, and stiffens her torso. She does not close her eyes but rolls them up as if trying to find something in the back of her skull. "Okay. There's a grandfather energy stepping forward. It doesn't have to necessarily be your grandfather, but it could have been an elderly male that could have been like a grandfather to you. Does this make sense?"

"Yes." Grandfathers on both sides of my family have died.

Placing her hand on her throat, Marguerite continues, "I feel a constriction of the throat. This could mean that he could have choked, there was a hanging, or he had some type of throat or stomach cancer? Did he have a tube placed somewhere in his body?"

56

My grandfather Lindell Paxton died from esophageal cancer. In the final week of his life, he was in the hospital and had drainage around his lung, a pleural effusion. This led to difficulty breathing, and his doctor placed a breathing tube in his chest.

I affirm Marguerite's question with a nod. My skeptical side tries to not be too enthusiastic. With every question she asks, I feel a tension between my hope and my cynicism. I visualize two clones of myself, each representing opposing feelings. When Marguerite asks a question that resonates with my experience, the hopeful self wants to jump up triumphantly, while the cynical self holds it down.

Marguerite senses my anxiety. "Are you okay?"

"Yes, this is just strange . . . but in a good way."

She laughs. "How do you think *I* feel, with all these dead people talking to me?" She braces the table and looks up again. "Yes. Okay. Okay. This man says that you are often misunderstood in your family. Would this be a fair assessment?"

Uh, yeah. My immediate reaction is to believe family members misunderstand me because of my sexual orientation, but my "grandfather" could also mean my choice of a profession. My father always tells me he can't wait until I'm done with my doctorate so I can send him a check every month. I try to explain to him that even though I'm going to school this long, I won't make a huge salary. I have an uncle who, no matter how much I explain my profession, still thinks I'm a psychologist. I was one of a few family members who decided to leave my hometown, and my Uncle Harry is the only family member who pursued education beyond a bachelor's degree. There could be many reasons I'm misunderstood.

Marguerite continues, "He wants me to tell you that he is proud of you and not to worry about what people think. Just keep doing what you're doing."

This does sound a lot like my Grandpa Lindell. He would come over to our house many nights during the week, to the point where my mother thought it was a little too much. In grade school, Grandpa Lindell would invite me out to dinner on Friday nights at a local restaurant with an all-you-can-eat fried chicken buffet. "You eat what you want," he'd say after we both had already finished two heaping plates full of Southern cooking. My stomach growls at the thought of those meals full of fried chicken, mashed potatoes and gravy, green beans, cornbread, and peach cobbler smothered in ice cream. After these dinners, I would then spend the night at his house. The next morning, Grandpa would buy two sacks of assorted donuts, one for him and one for me. I would eat the whole bag. I'm surprised that Marguerite hasn't mentioned the nicknames he used to call me, "Bullfrog Jack" and "Jack Rabbit." I'm not sure where these nicknames came from, but he used them until the day he died.

Maybe this information is too specific. I'm expecting too much.

Marguerite's next question snaps me back to attention. "Has your father died?"

I feel my eyebrows furrow together in concern. "No." *Oh, great. Here comes the wrong information.* I want to start accusing her of being a fraud.

"Hmm. He keeps talking about his son being with him. So I don't know if your father had a brother who passed?"

Confused from this inquiry, I'm about to give up faith in her abilities when it hits me. Grandpa Lindell was married to another woman before my grandmother, and he had three sons with her. My father was never close with his half brothers, and I only interacted with them a few times. I feel a chill when I remember that one of them died from pancreatic cancer two years ago.

After explaining this to Marguerite, she says, "It is interesting, because sometimes spirits offer information we are not expecting. Did your grandfather smoke anything? Because I smell cigar smoke."

For some reason, I begin to smell cigar smoke too. "Grandpa Lindell did not smoke, but my other deceased grandfather smoked cigars for years."

"There is a possibility that spirits can come through together at the same time—this is called piggybacking. He also says he is proud of you. Okay, okay." She stops and giggles. "I don't want to be offensive, but I want to state this like he is saying it. Are you somewhat of a geek?"

I laugh out loud. This sounds like something snarky my Grandpa Corky would have said—the same grandfather that lovingly called me the "Big Man on Campus." This was the man who took great pride in knowing that former president "Give 'em Hell" Harry S. Truman was his third cousin. He was the vain gentleman who colored his hair, but also annoyed my grandmother when he cleaned out his ears with his car keys. This grandfather was one you could never keep a straight face around, because he was always cracking a joke. Although possessing a strong sense of humor, he could also turn serious when one of his grandchildren engaged in an activity that he considered risky. I remember he had a fit at one of Kyle's birthday parties when Kyle received a four-wheel all-terrain vehicle for a gift. He had said to my parents, "I can't believe you bought that for him. He's going to break his neck!"

Responding to Marguerite's question, I affirm, "Yes. I am working on my PhD in communication, so I guess I'm somewhat of a geek."

Marguerite smiles. "This grandfather is also expressing how proud of you he is. They both are bragging about you a lot. 'Just keep doing what you're doing!' they say. The next energy coming through is someone who had an issue with the head."

Another chill goes up the back of my neck. *Could this be Mom?*

"This could be someone who died from blunt trauma to the head, shot in the head, a type of brain cancer. . . ."

"My deceased mother suffered from complications of a pituitary tumor."

"Okay. Was she the person you wanted to hear from the most today?"

"Yes."

"How do you connect with the number 12? This can refer to the 12th day of a month . . . 12 years . . . December being the 12th month of the year."

"She died in December." My heartbeat quickens, and I can hear my own pulse.

"I'm starting to feel like my breathing is labored. Do you know why this might be?"

"My mother had pituitary cancer, but her actual cause of death was a pulmonary embolism at home."

"Okay . . . Wow. This is odd. I'm also sensing there was something with her vision and the eyes."

I feel tears in the corners of my eyes. Marguerite grabs a tissue and hands it to me. "They couldn't get all of the tumor, because it was so close to her optic nerve," I confirm. "She had double vision before she died." *This is getting very strange.*

"Have you not told many people about this reading today?"

"I have told a few family members and friends." Almost all of my friends in Tampa know. I haven't told many family members and friends in my hometown, but I don't contact them often anyway. For some reason, I feel as though I'm betraying my father by not telling him that I'm here. As troubled as his marriage to my mother was, I know he loved her very much and thinks of her often. I wonder if I'll ever tell him about this experience. All of these aspects combined—my secrecy surrounding this reading, Marguerite's secluded office, and the cash-only payment policy—make me feel as if I'm completing an illegal drug deal.

"Okay . . . Okay . . . I understand." Marguerite is speaking off to the side now—as if my mother is standing next to her. "She's intrigued that I can hear her. She is adamant that you tell more people about this reading. She wonders why you haven't done a reading sooner."

Well, Mom, I don't always have $125.

"Do you have a brother?" Marguerite asks.

Wow. "Yes. I have a younger brother."

"She especially wants you to let him know about this. Your mother tells me that she is around both of you always. You *a lot* actually. . . Okay . . . Okay . . . She also is saying that at the end of her life she wasn't quite herself. The pain medicine she was on made her . . . loopy. Yes, 'loopy' is the word she is using. She doesn't mean all the harsh things she said."

Thinking about her final months of life, I do remember her being sharp with people. I can't remember anything hurtful that she might've said. I guess there are some negative memories of illness that the passage of ten years can erase. My relatives would often speak in hushed voices after one of her "Not Ann" moments and say, "That's the illness speaking."

Marguerite continues to focus on my mother's messages. "Were your father and mother separated or divorced before she died?"

"No. Why do you ask?" My mind flashes to a vision of Dad angrily shoving clothes in garbage bags. He and my mother were screaming at one another. I'm sure it was about money. This was the topic their arguments usually focused around. I remember my brother and me watching the scene unfold.

"That's it! I am getting the fuck out!" Dad yelled.

My mother began to unpack one of his bags. "Lindon! Stop it! You're upsetting the boys!"

After screaming matches, there was usually tense silence between them for days. Once, they went almost two weeks without talking. My mother would mischievously grin and say, "He thinks that when he doesn't talk to me it bothers me, but I really love it. Ha!"

I sigh as I contemplate this information. *At least Dad has improved in how he approaches conflict.*

I say to Marguerite, "They did fight a lot when I was growing up."

Marguerite nods. "Your mom was just saying something about them being at a crossroads, but she's fine. She has moved on. I think she might be trying to let your Dad know that it's okay that he has moved on too."

"Dad told me that after Mom died he kept having dreams with her in them. He would try to talk to her, but she always had her back turned to him. She would never speak to him. He has told me that he believed she was trying to tell him that he needed to move on."

"The deceased can come to us in dreams. She may have been telling him that. Now, her mother is still living. Yes?"

I nod.

Marguerite continues. "I feel that your grandmother took your mother's death very hard. She's had a history of anxiety problems, but once your mother died it seemed as if they got worse. Your mother is letting me know that she is around your grandmother often, and she would like you to tell her about this reading. She's also showing me a large bouquet of roses. When spirits show me this symbol, it can mean one of two things: either they were not very affectionate in life and they want to show you their unconditional love now, or it's just an extension of that from beyond."

"My mother was somewhat affectionate when she was alive."

"Okay. Good. She is telling me that she is happy that you are happy. I know this is a general statement, but maybe she is referring to something specific?"

"I am gay. I never got the chance to tell her."

Marguerite gives a few light slaps on the table. "Yes. The vibration is rising when you said that. I think that is what she is referring to."

I smile through tears. "That makes me feel wonderful." The cynical side of me retreats. "This experience has been amazing!"

"I'm glad you are enjoying it. You never know what to expect from the spirit world! Okay . . . Okay . . . Your mother is showing me a farm. Did you all live on a farm?"

"No, but my uncle and aunt, her sister, live on a farm. We spent a lot of time there."

"Okay. Yes, she's showing me a farm and horses. Did she like horses?"

"Everyone used to ride two of the horses in their backyard—everyone except me. I'm allergic to horses."

When I was about six years old, I was at a summer barbeque at Aunt Cindy and Uncle John's house. Many of my mother's siblings and their families were in attendance. We all took turns riding one of my aunt and uncle's horses, Beauty, in the backyard. Thirty minutes later, my mother found herself in my aunt's bathroom, frantically dousing me in a cool bubble bath. My body was bright red, itchy, and swollen. When the swelling wouldn't go down, she resorted to giving me liquid Benadryl, and this helped. She consulted with our family doctor, and we determined that I was allergic to horsehair.

This would be one of many medical crises my mother would have to attend to for members of my family: My brother as a toddler went into anaphylactic shock after eating peanut butter and crackers (due to an extreme allergy to peanuts). My father, while working underground in the coal mines, had a hammer slam back into his face, causing massive bone breakage. One summer night my brother, after playing outside all afternoon, came home urinating blood from a urinary tract infection. When I was a teenager, I worked at a hardware store and was rotating a giant truck tire. I stuck my hand in the wrong place and ended up splitting and fracturing the tip of my finger. As the nurses were sewing it closed on the operating table, I remember Mom rushing in and saying, "What the hell were you thinking?"

I stare at the small indention on my left index finger from the accident. For about three months after the stitches healed, this part of my finger was numb. I worried for so long that I would never feel anything again, but Mom reassured me that the feeling would return. In a peculiar way, this injury reminds me of my grief. Like Mom's death, the injury was sudden and unexpected. After trying to go through the various healing rituals, I felt numb for a while. Now, I still recognize my grief. I know the scar is there, the experience has marked me in particular ways, but I learn to live with it and the grief productively.

I find some of the signs Marguerite has brought up interesting. She continues to nod enthusiastically and smile. "The dead contact us often, but many people do not see these signs because they do not believe that afterlife communication can occur. It is wonderful that you and your family are open to these possibilities. Was your mother a model?"

"No. She was a hairdresser. If anything, she always was down on her looks. She had a lot of confidence in her wit and ability to interact with people, but she didn't think highly of her appearance. She especially didn't feel good about herself during her illness."

Marguerite snaps her fingers, which I notice are finely manicured with green polish. "Ah! That's it. She was saying something about being 'model material.' She is model material now!"

I chuckle and picture Mom doing a diva snap and saying, "Yeah! Who's sexy now?"

"Spirits can choose how they want me to see them," Marguerite adds. "Your mother is very beautiful. Perhaps she is showing herself to me in this way because she wants you to know that she is happy and at peace with her self-image."

"She was a beautiful woman, and I always wished she wasn't so down on herself."

Marguerite reaches out and places her hand on my arm. "Just know that she is at peace and around you all the time."

"I believe that death does not have to end a relationship with the deceased," I state. I unveil my academic identity and tell Marguerite about my research.

"This is all important work," she commends me, standing up from her chair. "I hate to tell you this, but I am feeling the energies pull back. Your reading has now officially ended."

I sigh, feeling satisfied but slightly disappointed, the same way you might feel upon finishing a great novel whose characters you were highly invested in. You know the author had to end the work eventually, but you're still left with questions. You still want to connect with the characters; you desire more.

As Marguerite walks me to her front door, she hands me a business card. "If you want to come back, don't hesitate to call. We don't have to do a reading, even if you just have questions about what I do."

"Thank you again for this. I appreciate it!" We exchange hugs.

On the drive home, I have much to think about. The sunny and breezy 70-degree weather on my commute along the Howard Frankland Bridge matches my mood. Rolling down the windows of my car and taking in a deep breath of ocean air, I smile as I feel the wind blow in my face. No matter how many times I drive over this bridge, I never tire of seeing the Tampa city skyline and the glimmer of sunshine reflecting on the bay.

One of the many aspects that I still appreciate about my mother was her willingness to encourage me to do whatever I was passionate about. When she was in high school, she was on the school dance team, the pep squad, and the home economics club. She went to beauty school to be a hairdresser. This was different from what I chose to do and what I do with my career. I never envisioned myself being a professor, but I can imagine she would be proud of me. After the psychic reading, I have more faith in this belief.

Although I thought Marguerite could have been more specific on some details, I don't think she was completely off. For instance, she didn't ask if I had lost a spouse or a sibling. Unfortunately, my cynical side wants to trivialize the experience. *There are many things she could have guessed about you. From the beginning, when she asked if you had a grandfather "figure" who died, it could have been a scam. Either way, if you had a grandfather die or not, you would come up with someone to connect with her question.*

My hopeful side responds. *You're right. Still, I think the reading was worth the time and the money.*

Even if the reading was not "real" in the objective sense, it still had a lot of meaning for me. It helped me remember details about both my grandfathers and my relationships with them that I had forgotten about. Most importantly, I continued a bond with my mother through the reading, and it strengthened my appreciation for the time that we shared and all the work she did to make sure my brother and I had the best childhoods possible.

Marguerite stated that people often miss messages from the dead because they haven't opened themselves up to the possibility of the dead being able to communicate. However, after today, and after learning about continuing bonds, I intend to keep my eyes fully open.

I also intend to return to DuQuoin for a visit.

CHAPTER 3

HOME

"On the way to get away from where you are, you can run so fast that you miss the blessings along the way. By the time you realize that you have missed them, a major portion of your life has taken place without you."

As I sit on the plane traveling to my hometown, I read the statement once again. Spiritual guru Iyanla Vanzant's (2012) message resurrects the thoughts that haunt me. The statement opens my personal Pandora's box of ghosts. The ghosts beckon me out of Flight 1270 and into a deep sea of unfinished business. I am bewitched. The ghosts move my fingers across the keyboard, and from this exorcism come my anxieties over having abandoned those I love.

In my rush to get away from the constraints of my rural hometown, did I miss something? Was the pain from the loss of my mother too much to bear? Did I fear rejection for being gay so much that this fear motivated me to lose connections with the people who mattered most?

I will be home for twelve days.

It's still hard to comprehend. The last time I was home for this long was on winter break during my first semester of graduate school. That trip lasted a numbing nine days—fixed behind a television set, just waiting to go back to Tampa.

I realize now why this last trip had made me feel numb.

It was because I hadn't tried.

On that last visit home, I didn't have many conversations with my father, stepmother, and younger brother. We talked to one another, but we didn't *connect*. Familial soap operas and shame created a dark cloud of severed ties. Evening sitcoms became hiding places. I could hide from admitting the truth. I could hide from my sexuality. I could hide from my grief over my mother's death. Belly laughs, cackles, and snickers from every joke became a shield that helped keep the things we were afraid of from coming in. We kept the terrors at bay, and they prevented us from intimate moments of physical touch and emotional consolation.

I didn't have the sitcoms to protect myself from my grandmother. I had to physically separate myself from her. I made a conscious effort to not visit her alone. If I did, I would've had to talk about my mother's death. I would've had to console her. *I wish she wasn't so depressing. I wish she would just get over it*, I would think. I realize now she was seeking help. She wanted her favorite grandson to sit with her, watch Oprah, and talk. She wanted to remember and re-establish a connection with my mother.

And I shut her out.

Maybe I wasn't willing to face the pain of the loss. Maybe I feared that if Grandma crumbled, I would too. I was a fighter. I had already faced discrimination and hatred for being a gay man—which, for some individuals, indicated that I was weak. Shed not a tear, you big queer. I wasn't going to lose in this fight for self-preservation. So, I ignored my grandmother.

I also shut out family friends and neighbors. What would they think about me now? How could I face that? The day of my mother's death? Seeing them would put me back in that hell—the hell of watching her take her last breath.

I'm not sure why I had these negative thoughts about my community. Maybe they stemmed from my past. The taunts from schoolyard bullies had now turned into whispered gossip among adults in grocery stores. People will talk—especially in a small town. I imagine middle-aged women saying: "Is that Blake? That's the boy whose mother died so tragically years ago? He was always such a sweet boy. He has lost so much weight. Do you think he's anorexic? I heard that he's a queer. Maybe he has AIDS? His poor father! He must be so disappointed." Or they might say: "He went to live in the city. Look at him. He thinks he is better than us!"

Even in my head, I just can't help but feel the sting that comes from scrutinizing eyes. To me, at every turn in DuQuoin—in every store, in the park, and in the town square—there's the threat of being the subject of small-town musings.

And so, in the past when I visited DuQuoin, I stayed in my family home as much as possible. It was a safe haven. It was a place I could ride out the storm—to hide from rejection and from the unbearable pain of loss.

I keep having another nightmare. No one dies in this dream. There's no monster or boogeyman. I'm teaching speech in my old high school. After ten years of postsecondary education, a PhD, and almost $100,000 in student loans, I see myself as the target of paper airplanes and spit wads from immature teenagers.

There is something telling about the dream. No matter how much I try to escape the past, it will catch up with me. I can never leave it behind, and I have to deal with it being in me.

And I have a project to complete.

* * *

Today marks the ten-year anniversary of my mother's death. I think about this as I sit in the same recliner she sat in before she stopped breathing. This is the same recliner that I sat in after the funeral when I stared at the devastated faces of my younger brother and my father. This is the same recliner I watched my father fall asleep in every night after strained silence between us, when I would think *How are we ever going to move on with life?*

Gagging down my bitter lukewarm coffee, I contemplate the possibility of my first day of winter vacation. The television drones on with mindless morning talk show babble. My younger brother, father, and stepmother are at work. The house feels cold and deserted. Never faring well in an unfamiliar bed, my sore body feels the aftermath of tossing and turning through an almost sleepless night. I wonder if this is how Mom felt on those lonely mornings when we were all gone. It saddens me to remember the pain of her illness in her final months.

Attempting to shake away the dreary memories, I push myself out of the recliner. While washing my breakfast dishes, I call my Aunt Jan, Mom's older sister. She works at an adult senior citizen center in my hometown. I ask her if my grandma (my mother's mother) will be there today.

"Hey, bud! I didn't realize you would be home so soon," she says with surprise. "Grandma Jo-Ann will be eating lunch at about eleven fifteen. Everybody usually visits and watches the news for about an hour afterwards. So I think if you get here about noon you should catch her."

"Okay, thanks. I'll see you soon."

"Oh, and Blake?"

"Yeah?"

"You do realize today is the day, right?"

Of course today is the day, I think. *How can you ever forget the day you lost your mother—the most important person in your life? It's burned into my brain.*

"I know," I respond.

"I still can't believe it. She was too young." Her voice cracks. "But she was in so much pain. I guess God needed someone to do hair for him."

I smile and sigh.

"I guess so," I say.

"But you know how Chickee can be." Chickee is the nickname Mom and her sisters made for my grandma. They don't address her as Chickee, but she's aware of the nickname.

Jan continues, "She'll want to have a sob session."

I stiffen. This statement is something *I* would have said in the past. It's something I would have said to further distance myself from my grandmother.

"Don't worry about it. I study grief now. I'm prepared if Grandma wants to talk about Mom. It will probably be good for us."

"Okay. I'll help you out if you need it," Jan says.

I hang up, put the dishes away, and prepare for my visit.

* * *

I enter the senior citizen center and am cheerfully greeted by a receptionist at the front desk.

"I'm looking for my grandma . . . Jo-Ann Strong?"

The receptionist takes a moment to examine me. After she has determined that I'm not a threat, she nods her head to the right, behind the desk. "She should be in the dining hall. They just finished their lunch."

As I enter the room, a musty scent mixed with chicken broth creeps up my nostrils. I see a few of the residents finishing their lunch. After close inspection of a few plates, I discover the menu of the day: chicken and dumplings, mashed potatoes and gravy, green beans, and a roll. It would be appetizing if the physical setting of the dining room didn't remind me of a middle school cafeteria. I think about times as a kid when I fed myself school entrees like dry pizza, cold and soggy French fries, and chocolate milk. I remember kids chewing with their mouths open and playing with their food—creating mixed concoctions like canned corn and Jell-O. My stomach churns as I remember stuffing myself with that awful food and then running around for thirty minutes at recess almost making myself puke. All of these moments make me sick when I smell the seniors' lunch for the day. I try to block the scents to keep my nausea at bay.

The dining room consists of three rows of long metal tables. There are only a couple of individuals who remain seated at the tables—a heavy-set black man in overalls and a petite white woman with a tight, frizzy perm of gray hair. Multicolored Christmas lights are strung along the walls. Farther past the tables is a sitting room for the center's visitors to socialize. It consists of a circle of worn armchairs and sofas aimed at a large screen television.

I spot my eighty-two-year-old grandmother, hunched over her walker. Osteoporosis has taken its toll on her body. She shakes as she slowly moves the walker in front of her. I notice how clearly the bones protrude from her hands as she grips the walker. Even though it's only been a year since I've seen her, I can't help but notice how aged she looks. I don't think I'm afraid of getting older, but it distresses me to think about her having to walk half bent over. I try to imagine this sensation, mixed with the feelings of constant aches and pains. *What will the experience of growing old be like? Will people visit me?*

I brush my thoughts aside, walk up behind her, and lightly tap her shoulder. I'm not sure how she'll react. Maybe she'll be upset with me because I never call. Maybe she won't even recognize me. "Grandma?"

She turns and is taken aback. Her mouth drops open in a surprised smile.

"Well, my word! I knew you were coming to town but didn't think you'd already be here. How are you, sweetie?"

My fears of rejection and uncertainty melt away. I give her a tight embrace, but not too tight. "I'm great. I arrived last night."

"I'm going to the restroom. Take a seat. I'll be back."

She carefully inches the walker in front of her as she approaches the restroom door. As if in an awkward dance, I keep turning to look at the row of chairs and back at her. *Does she need my help?* This must be what an anxious father feels like when watching his child walk for the first time.

After deciding that she'll be fine, I take a seat on one of the sofas and wait for her return. I gaze around at the center's residents. A few of the women smile at me. One man is staring catatonically into space. One lady quietly sings as she knits a scarf.

When my grandma returns, I help her take a seat next to me on the sofa. After getting situated, she takes a deep breath and says, "So when did you get in, hon?"

"I arrived late last night. I flew into St. Louis and took the shuttle to Illinois. Dad picked me up and drove me home." The nearest airport to my hometown is ninety miles away in St. Louis.

"Your dad didn't pick you up from the airport?"

"No . . . you know how he feels about city traffic."

"I don't give a damn! You're not here that often. The least he could do was pick you up at the airport."

I feel a tense silence. My father and grandmother have never been the best of friends. I'm thankful when she changes the subject.

"So where are you in your program?"

"I'm in the second year of the PhD program. I teach interpersonal communication to the undergraduates. I should be done in a few years."

"Well, that's just wonderful! I'm proud of you! You know when you kids were growing up, you always had your nose in a book. I remember your mom talking about you and your brother. She'd say, 'I got one who I can't ever track down and I got one who I can't ever get his ass out of the house.'"

I laugh. "I was definitely the reader! It helps to be one in graduate school. Sometimes I have to read three books in one week!"

There's a lull in our conversation, and then comes the moment I've prepared for. "You know, it'll be ten years today," she murmurs.

"Yes. I know," I say.

I tell Grandma about my research. I tell her about how we can continue relationships with those who have died even though they're no longer physically with us.

She responds, "It's great that you're doing this research about your mom. I think about her every day. God love her. Out of all my kids, she never mouthed me. You know she would give me her opinion, but she never got rude. Such a gentle soul."

I let out a sigh. "I think about her and talk to her every day. I even have pictures in my apartment in Tampa. While I'm home, I want to see if I can find her old appointment book. Do you remember that thing?"

My grandmother laughs. "Yes! I don't know how the hell she ever read her handwriting. And there were hair-color smudges all over it."

HOME

"I'm going to go to her grave while I'm home."

"You should. When's the last time you were there?"

"I'm not sure. Maybe five or six years?"

"I go when I can. Sometimes your Aunt Cindy will take me there. I feel closer to your mom there."

"There's a psychic I've been watching named Theresa Caputo. She says that our loved ones are always with us. We think we have to go to their graves to visit them, but she says that's not the case. They are always around."

"I believe that. It's hard, though. I miss your mom and your grandpa. . ."

She starts to sob.

I take her into my arms and hold her head close to my chest. I want to hold her tightly—to reassure her that I'll be strong for her. But I fear injuring her fragile body. And then I think, *Why do I have to be strong?* Instead of me being some solid rock she can hold on to, maybe in this moment we can hold on to our grief together.

When we release from the embrace, I pull some tissues from my pocket. As I slowly wipe her tears, I start to feel my own tears.

"I'm such a mess," Grandma says.

"Me too. We're both a big hot mess!" I say.

We chuckle. Then, there's a brief silence.

Sometimes in spaces of grief, silence is what we need.

"I still catch myself picking up the phone to call her," Grandma says. "I know it's silly. I can't talk to her."

"But you *can* talk to her, Grandma. You shouldn't ever feel strange for having a conversation with her or Grandpa. I wouldn't recommend trying to call either of them on the phone, though."

Grandma laughs. "You're funny—just like your mom. Did I ever tell you the story about her walking around the pews on Easter Sunday in her new dress?"

"No. What happened?"

"She was six years old, and we had bought her a bright yellow dress for Easter. She loved it. We're sitting in church on Easter Sunday during Mass. With seven kids, it's hard to keep track of everyone. I thought your grandpa was keeping an eye on her. Little did I know that she started prancing up and down the aisles. She kept saying to people, 'Look at my pretty dress! Isn't it pretty?' And she was curtseying. It was the cutest thing, but it was in the middle of the service. I had to walk to the back of the church to get her."

It's such a small story, but it means so much. Since my mother died, I've heard many stories about her adulthood. The childhood tales have seemed to disappear, but I know that it's possible to bring them back. It's possible to piece together the fragments of my mother's past. It's possible to continue a relationship with her and encourage others to continue this relationship.

I leave the senior citizen center feeling elated. I realize that all the times I ignored my grandmother in fear that she would bring up Mom's death, I was missing out on the beauty of our relationship. I realize that even though she's eighty-four years old, I can still make up for lost time. It's not too late to continue a bond with her through my mother's legacy.

* * *

I must visit Mom.

Never having felt so compelled, I'm not sure why I have such a strong desire to go to the cemetery. Maybe the visit with my grandmother has made me realize that I can be immersed in grief. Maybe this is another test I have given myself—a test to see if I can quit running away from my past and face the pain of loss I've evaded for ten years.

All of these thoughts swirl in my mind as I drive the family Ford Expedition through town. This was "her" car. The license plate used to read LABKM98 (L stood for my father, Lindon. A stood for my mother, Ann. B stood for me, Blake. K stood for my brother, Kyle. M stood for our dog, Maddie. 1998 was the year my parents bought the car). The license plate has been replaced and now reads a random number.

I hear a familiar country song on the radio, a song Mom and I used to sing together. Driving in "her" car takes me back to some fond memories. My mother was a wild driver—a conservative motorist might have called her reckless. On my twelfth birthday she took my best friend and me out to dinner and a movie. I, being the "nerd" as she called me with sarcastic affection, insisted we visit the local bookstore before the movie. While they waited on me, she sped through the parking lot, aiming the car at the numerous birds gathered there. I think about her speeding through the lot yelling, "Wahoo!" and the birds scattering for their lives.

Whether it was from her intentionally swerving back and forth, pulsating the brakes, or speeding, Mom's passengers often had to grab the

HOME

handles located above the window—the "Oh shit!" handles, as we used to call them. On one occasion, Mom got out of a ticket by telling the police officer she was rushing to get home because she thought she was going to crap her pants. I remember her saying, "I wasn't sexy enough to flirt my way out of the ticket, so I had to play sick."

My mom was the person who taught me how to drive a car. My father didn't have much patience with drivers, especially his driver-in-training son, and so I was forced to put up with Mom's antics and practical jokes. I would get so angry, because she would periodically tickle me while I was trying to drive. "What are you going to do when a girl does that on a date?" she would ask, with a mischievous twinkle in her eye.

She would be proud that I've mastered the task of multitasking while driving, I think, *even if my dates are with men and not women.*

A car horn snaps me out of my nostalgia, and I realize that I've been sitting at a green light. I speed forward on my mission to visit the cemetery, but in my haste I've neglected one thing. I'm not sure where I'm going. *Which cemetery is Mom buried in?*

I search for "cemeteries in DuQuoin" on my phone and am surprised to see how many results there are. You would think in a town of six thousand people there wouldn't be that many cemeteries. *Sacred Heart Cemetery. That one sounds right.*

When I arrive, the place is deserted. It's the middle of a Tuesday afternoon, in winter. The nausea I felt at the senior center returns. I propel myself out of the car and vomit on the side of the road. After a round of coughing and puking, I pick myself up off the ground. I find some tissues in the glove compartment and clean myself up.

Why am I so unsettled? Do I want to get this test of grief "over with?" I've never experienced this sense of anxiety before. I feel disoriented and weak as I trudge between the rows of graves. My legs are shaking like Jell-O. The cool air is making my nose run and making the after-vomit-mucus dry around my eyes and lips. *Ugh,* I think. *I feel so disgusting.* My head throbs, and a headache forms, reminiscent of the kind that can develop from eating ice cream too quickly.

Trying my best to continue, I scan the names on the graves. *Emerson, James, Alongi. Where the hell is Paxton?* I get angry. *This is pathetic. You can't find your own mother's grave.*

I pause. "Just breathe," I tell myself, and I soon realize that this is the wrong cemetery.

My mother was buried in Cudgetown Cemetery, about a half a mile down the road. I get back in the car and drive to the correct space. When I arrive, I breathe a sigh of relief, and some of my anxiety diminishes. The scenery of this place rings true, and I find that I know where her grave is. It's almost as if my mother's spirit takes me by the hand and leads me to her grave.

It's next to my Grandma and Grandpa Paxton's grave. My father's future grave is already etched in place. Someone has left a bouquet of violet flowers—my mother's favorite color. I read the headstone:

ANN ELIZABETH PAXTON
April 29, 1964–December 19, 2004

Choking back sobs, I drop to my knees. It has been ten years, but it still hurts! I can't stand being in this cemetery, in my hometown, and in the house I grew up in. But I have to be in all of these places. *I must.* How can I ever grow or connect or rebuild from this loss if I don't immerse myself in spaces of pain? How can I ever transform my relationships? How can I ever become a better person if I keep running from my past? I can't move *on* from the loss of my mother, but I can move *through* it. I can learn how to hold it with me.

I pride myself on being able to continue a bond with my mother, but yet the hard gravestone makes me come to terms with the hard reality—*that she is physically gone.* I miss her touch. I miss her scent. I miss her voice the most. I yearn for her singing in the kitchen on Sunday afternoons as she fixes dinner. I yearn for her high-pitched cackle after cracking some self-deprecating joke. I even long to hear her yell some of the obscenities she was notoriously known for getting away with in front of more conservative family members and friends. *This* is the voice I know and the woman I love. Since I can't have her as a material entity, I settle for the next best option. I maintain a relationship with her spirit, because I still have a lot to live for. I know I have a purpose in life, and she wouldn't want me to give up.

But I still need to cry.

Alone in a deserted cemetery on a Tuesday afternoon, I'm left with a stone. I'm left with stories. I'm left with memories. I'm left with suspensions of disbelief.

HOME

Wiping my burning, chapped face, I say to the stone—to *her*— "Mom. . . I miss you so goddamn much! I love you and I know you're here. I know it. But maybe you can give me a sign that you're okay? Can you do that for me?"

Silence.

I walk away hoping that she'll respond.

* * *

I'm not sure why I'm nervous. It's a few days after my cemetery visit, and I'm ready to conduct my first interview for this project. After parking the car, I sit for a few minutes and breathe slowly, stalling my participation. Maybe I'm feeling anxious from driving on icy roads for the first time in two years. The winter climate of my hometown in southern Illinois is quite different from the sunny Florida weather to which I've become accustomed. Also, driving the family SUV is like navigating an ocean liner.

I wipe away a tear. *Get yourself together. You have an interview to do.* In an attempt to distract myself from my grief, I run through my personal research checklist to make sure I have all my supplies. *Digital recorder. Check. Interview schedule. Check. Tissues? Oh, damn. No tissues!*

How could I forget tissues? I'm interviewing seven of my mother's closest friends from her high school graduating class about her death, and I didn't bring any tissues? *The women may carry tissues in their purses,* I think. Then I remind myself, *That is such a gender stereotype!*

I take a deep breath and get out of the car, but when I approach the entrance of the Mexican restaurant where I'm supposed to meet the women, I feel my legs shaking. As I walk through the front door, the heat and smell of deep-fried tortilla chips calms me. Whenever I return to my hometown, this restaurant is always at the top of my list for dinners with friends and family.

The women are seated at a long table in the back of the restaurant. As I walk toward them, seven pairs of eyes move in my direction. Some of the women smile, and others exude expressions of uncertainty. These seven are middle-class white women around the age of 50—what would have been my mother's age. I know half of them (Jill, Kristy, Kathy, and Jean Ann) fairly well but have had little interaction with the others (Shannon, Shelley, and Susan).

75

My nerves are soothed when Jill yells, "Hey, Blake!" I smile upon hearing the slight hint of a familiar Southern drawl.

"We've saved a seat for you!" Kristy says and gestures to the seat on her right.

"Thank you all for agreeing to do this," I say as I sit down. "I know it can be difficult for everyone to get together around the holidays."

As we munch on stale tortilla chips and watery salsa, we make small talk. Kristy passes around an album of her daughter Jessica's engagement pictures. Jessica was in my high school graduating class, and while I had heard from my family about her engagement, she and I haven't spoken in years. The ladies "ooh" and "ahh" admiringly over the pictures. I feel a little discomfort, because Jessica is my age and already done with her degree, in a career she loves, and engaged to what sounds like a great man. My discomfort increases when Jill turns to me and asks, "Do you have a boyfriend, Blake?"

I had assumed none of them would be so direct with this question, although the love lives of town residents are often popular topics of conversation. In the past, my sexual orientation often seems to constrain these discussions from happening. People either avoid the subject entirely, or they assume I'm straight and ask, "Have you found a woman yet?"

"No. I am so busy with this PhD it is difficult to date," I respond.

Across the table, I spot Shannon digging through her purse. She seems distant and distracted. "I got to go smoke a cigarette," she states and quickly departs.

I sense she's uncomfortable. From the moment I entered the room, I couldn't help but notice her troubled expression. Her pursed lips and piercing glare was not the face of the Shannon I was used to growing up. *What have I done to upset her?*

There is an awkward silence.

Kristy turns and pats my shoulder. "Sorry, Blake. Shannon never took your mother's death well."

Shelley adds, "Shannon always thought more could be done. . . that we didn't try enough."

I sigh. "There wasn't anything else anybody could do."

Jill nervously stirs her drink. "She was hesitant to do this interview."

Jean Ann interjects, "Jill. He doesn't have to know that. We're happy to help, Blake."

What am I doing here? I think. *I never want to force anyone to do anything for my research.* "We could have done this another night. I don't want her to do this if it will be difficult for her."

Jill shakes her head. "No. . . no. . . after we talked to her, she agreed that it would be good for her. Let her release some steam, and when she gets back, we'll get started."

Within a couple minutes, Shannon returns with the same tense expression. I hesitantly explain my research project. "Again, I don't want you to feel like you have to do this," I say. "I want this project to help people, not make them feel worse."

Shannon responds quickly, "I am doing this because I loved your mom. I may not understand you and your gay lifestyle, but I want to help."

Her statement is strikingly direct. "Thanks, Shannon." I respond softly. This is all I can offer. I'm not in the proper context to discuss my "lifestyle" with her. Any time I get frustrated in situations such as these, I often remember what a good friend told me once. He said, "Think about how long it took *you* to accept that you were gay. Do you expect your loved ones to adjust immediately?" He made a great point, and it often gives me comfort. I hope this will be a successful interview, despite the tension.

The women continue to listen attentively as I explain my project. I try to ignore the background noise of the restaurant—servers yelling in Spanish, men laughing and clinking beer bottles, and mariachi music over a built-in speaker.

I turn on the recorder, and Jill asks, "You sure you have enough space on your recorder? You know how much we can talk!" The women giggle and converse among themselves.

I laugh. "Oh yes, up to three hours. But I don't imagine this taking that long."

The recorder further accentuates my peculiar positioning in this interactional experience. It's a symbol of the tension felt from insider/outsider status in ethnographic research. I want this experience to be a conversation among my mother's friends, but at the same time, I want "good data" to represent the complexity in our lived experiences of grief and loss. I wish to make the research process more collaborative with interviewees, and I don't feel comfortable taking on the role of a detached researcher. But by asking questions that might prompt displays of grief, am I like a mad scientist who creates certain conditions in order to test subjects in an experiment?

I brush these thoughts aside and focus again on the interview. "Could you each tell me how you met my mother and how you came to be friends? Also, feel free to share a story about her."

Jill eagerly jumps in, "Ann went to the Catholic grade school with Kristy. I was not a close friend with your mom until high school. We were both on the school dance team. I have a couple stories that will show you who Ann was."

The stories flow. Jill laughs about her and Mom's teenage shopping woes. "We were both heavier in school. We'd go shopping, and we'd bitch because we couldn't find anything that fit. So, after we were done, you know what we'd do? Ann would say, 'Screw this! We're going to Dairy Queen to get ice cream!'"

I chuckle. "That sounds like Mom."

Jean Ann says, "She could always make you laugh. Make you laugh until you cried!"

Kristy adds, "Sometimes it was at her own expense, though. She could take the crummiest situation and make the best out of it. She knew how to make us feel better."

A few more stories about high school are exchanged, and then the women begin focusing on the cruise they all took for their fortieth birthdays. My mother went on the cruise to the Bahamas in April 2004. She died the following December. I remember her telling stories about the cruise, but I can't remember many of the details. Gratitude for the friendship these women brought my mother swells as I listen to them talk about their experiences on the trip.

Jean Ann tells me about how she and Mom got stuck sharing the top bunk in one of the rooms. Jean Ann struggles to get through her story because of laughter. "We made fun of ourselves! We were like, 'Here we go! Let's get our fat asses up here on this bunk!' We slept in little T-shirts and panties, and your mom made comments about our big butts and snoring! She joked about everything on that trip! Such a hoot!"

Kathy agrees. "She even made jokes about all the medicine she had to take for her illness. There was one time we were all on the beach. She had this huge plastic bag of pills in one hand and a drink in the other. She was like, 'I'm not supposed to be drinking with all these meds, but I don't give a shit! I'm on this trip and I'm going to have fun, goddamn it!'"

Shelly interjects, "That's Ann!"

Jean Ann adds, "Yeah, she cursed like a sailor. You knew there'd always be a 'Fuck you!' in there somewhere."

Jill says, "But she always got away with it somehow."

We laugh hysterically, and I realize that our tears are not so much a result of sadness but of laughter.

After a moment, I state, "I want to tell you all that I appreciate the friendship you gave my mother. She had so much fun on that trip." My voice cracks.

Their faces are full of sympathy. I manage to choke out, "I'm glad she got to go on that trip before she died. It was probably one of the best experiences of her life."

Kristy's eyes glisten as she puts her hand on my shoulder. "Your mom would be so proud of you and your brother."

"Thanks," I respond as I take one of the table napkins and wipe my tears.

Kathy says, "We see so much of your mom in you, Blake. . ." There is an abrupt pause. She begins to cry. "I didn't realize this would be so hard." She forks out tissues from her handbag and dabs her eyes. Jill gives Kathy a hug and nuzzles her head against Kathy's forehead.

"I am so sorry," I say. "I don't mean to upset you."

Kathy shakes her head. "Oh, no. It's fine! I'm just being a hormonal middle-aged woman!"

Sensing a break in the tension, I find a good time to move the conversation in another direction. "Do you think it's possible to continue a relationship with Mom even though she's not physically here?"

Many of the women nod their heads in agreement.

Susan proclaims, "I still go to her grave on Memorial Day and whenever I can."

I'm appreciative that Susan does this, but I wonder whether any of Mom's friends do things outside of traditional memorializing practices. A peculiar feeling of guilt overwhelms me. Not only have I asked questions that have resulted in tears, but also I feel that I'm pressuring these women to memorialize my mother. If they think they've moved on from the loss, is this acceptable? People continue to live their lives when someone dies, and just because they don't memorialize or re-member that person doesn't mean they didn't love or care about the person. I want them to know about the variety of options for re-membering rituals should they choose to participate in them.

"Are there formal rituals that you do to memorialize Mom?" I ask.

Susan laughs. "We're not formal people." She and the other women pause for a few moments.

"There was that one time at Mickey's," Susan says. "It's our favorite steakhouse in Florida, and they have hundreds of dollar bills on the walls. We made one out to your mom, and we always look for it when we go there."

This is a good start. Maybe it will help if I explain more about my research interests. I explain the history of the continuing bonds literature and what exactly re-membering rituals entail. This seems to stimulate conversation.

Kristy smiles and reminisces about peanut rolls. "When your mom and I were young, we would spend time at my grandmother's house. While we were there, we would often make peanut rolls. I remember when I heard that your mom died, I tried to go to work the next day. My supervisor sent me home because she could see that I was distraught. When I got home, I just kept making peanut rolls. I made over six dozen! I make them every year now, and I always think about your mom and my grandma when I make them."

I smile.

Shannon adds, "I think a lot of how we continue a relationship with Ann is through our continued commitment to get together at Christmas and go on trips. My mom always says she doesn't know how we can get together after all these years and still have stuff to talk about."

Kathy says, "And we can always pick up where we left off. We don't have to explain our family situations to each other."

Jean Ann proudly exclaims, "We can just be ourselves!"

Kristy turns to me. "At our last class reunion, our husbands stated that they wished they planned trips with their friends. We were like, 'You got to make the effort!'"

I laugh. As I reflect on these moments, I find that this interview is serving as a re-membering ritual for Mom. I can see that they are proud to be who they are—proud to be rural women. In this moment, it's almost as if this re-membering ritual is also a form of feminist consciousness-raising. Through reflecting on my mother's strength, it seems, her friends feel a sort of female empowerment. I also feel empowered and proud— proud to be in this moment with them, proud of the profound dedication to their friendship with each other and my mother, and proud of where I came from. My preconceived notions about rejection and fear of my hometown community seem trivial now.

The transformative and inspirational nature of this interview is summed up best when Shelley says, "Your mother's death definitely made us realize how precious life is and how important it is to continue our friendship."

I turn to all of them and raise my glass, "Well said, Shelley. Thank you all! Let's give a toast to Ann!"

After the toast, the rest of the evening is spent taking pictures and sharing more stories—stories about other loves and losses. The hum of small-town chatter invigorates me. I smile as I watch the women instruct one another on how to change the font size of text messages on their phones; I get choked up again when I think about what it would be like if Mom were still here. But I realize that after all of the stories and laughter, she *is* here. I can't change the past, but I can make the best of the present. After this evening, I further understand the ability to hold joy and sorrow together, and I know that my mother's friends do as well. As we re-member my mother, I re-member myself back into the community I left behind.

Later, when I'm walking to my car in the parking lot, Shannon approaches me. "Blake, I apologize if I was harsh earlier."

"It's okay, Shannon," I respond.

"I have a cousin who came out as gay recently. It is hard for me to understand. I'm trying."

"I know."

Before I can say another word, she gives me a hug. Her kind act leaves me speechless. Immersed in our grief, there's the potential for finding a way to accept the other we thought we did not understand.

* * *

"You want to watch *what*?"

My younger brother, Kyle, is skeptical. The events of the last week have inspired me to continue participating in rituals of re-membering Mom and to include other family members in these activities.

Even though only four years separate us in age, the relationship I have with my brother hasn't always been the most loving. I tell people that we're as different as night and day. Kyle was the star athlete. He struggled in school but was dynamite on the football field. Today, he chews and spits tobacco, talks about pretty women, and usually wears an old pair of jeans, flannel shirt, ball cap, and work boots. In contrast,

I have never touched tobacco, talk about gorgeous men, and try to keep up with the latest fashion trends. I was the smart child—as Kyle sometimes bitterly described me. He was open about his jealousy of my being a straight A student, and he would sometimes start physical fights with me because of this jealousy.

However, after Mom died we became closer. We had to help each other fill the painful silences in the evenings after school—times when we, along with my father, would sit catatonically in front of the television set privately hoping Mom would come walking through the front door. It was difficult, but we survived.

It's no surprise that he's hesitant when I ask him to view the photo slide show that was played at our mother's visitation service ten years ago. He grudgingly agrees, and I set my laptop on the bed. I slide the DVD of the show into the drive, and we wait with anticipation. We begin hearing soft piano music, and then the slides begin. We laugh when we see Mom and Dad in old school dance pictures. Mom is sporting a tight-knit '80s perm, and Dad is without a beard and has a haircut like John Travolta in *Saturday Night Fever*. The beautiful memories encapsulated through photographs keep coming: Mom cutting my hair in her salon when I was six, her posing with my brother in his uniform on the football field, and her with her friends on the birthday cruise.

I look at my brother and he's crying. I take his rough, callused hand in mine, and we finish watching the film. When it's over, we don't say anything. I take him in my arms, and we hug each other tightly. Our differences and the geographical distance that separates us don't matter in this moment. We feel grief in the silence, and in our silent grief, I realize our love.

* * *

Christmas Day has finally arrived. I wake up to find that, sadly, it hasn't snowed. There are reports of snow coming later in the evening, up to a foot in some places. Mom would be pleased. Every time I see snow, I think of her. While others might bemoan the extra physical labor that comes with excessive snowfall, I embrace the snow's childlike innocence and the potential to reconnect with Mom.

My brother and I decide to go to my cousin Ryan's house to visit with my mother's side of the family. When we arrive, I observe that not much has changed since last year. The large-screen television blares in the front room. Most of the men congregate around it, taking in a basketball game. Beers in hand, they shout cheerful greetings as we walk through the front door. Most of the women congregate in the kitchen and dining room area.

Typical of this side of the family, everyone starts speaking loudly and at once. I look around at the room of guests: Ryan, my grandmother, Aunt Cindy, Aunt Patty, Aunt Jan, Aunt Susie, my cousin Olivia, and my cousin Seth. I find the right place to interject in this chorus of family ruminations and tell my family about my psychic reading with Marguerite a few months ago. "It was pretty cool," I say.

Aunt Cindy responds, "I still connect with your mom. I have received many signs from her. I've told you that story about the balloon, haven't I?"

"Yes," I say.

My cousin Seth asks, "Wait—what happened, Mom?"

Everyone's attention is captured as Aunt Cindy narrates the story:

"I have witnesses to this event. I'm not just some menopausal woman! Ever since this happened, I believe that our loved ones are watching us from the other side and they can send us messages.

"It was your brother's birthday, May 31. It was the May after your mom had passed away. It was a cool day, and I had the windows open in the house. The sky was overcast with lots of thick clouds, and it looked like it could rain.

"The grandkids were over at the house. I had finished jamming to the radio while cleaning our swimming pool. My husband was fixing dinner on the grill, and I told everyone that I was going inside to fix a salad. As I was prepping the vegetables, I was feeling sad. I knew it was your brother's birthday, and I was thinking about how hard it must be to not have his mamma. I was also thinking about the previous May. Your mom had to have surgery on his last birthday. He was so little, and he did not understand why it had to be done on *his* day.

"All of a sudden, my two grandsons come running inside. Their eyes were as wide as silver dollars. You might have thought they had found gold. They started yelling, 'Grandma! Grandma! Look what we found!' One of them hands me a deflated balloon. A picture of a girl in a bed is on the front, and there is a message that says 'Dear God, please help my friend.'

"'Where did you find this?' I asked them. They told me they were playing in the backyard and saw the balloon fall from the sky. I looked at the bottom of the balloon, where the artist had signed her name: ANNIE.

"I said, 'This must be a sign from Sis!' You know everyone used to call her 'Annie,' so that was unique to her. As soon as I said that, the song 'Live Like You Were Dying' came on the radio. That song was popular when your mom was sick. She used to say, 'Oh, that's my song. I'm going to die!' I tried to tell her to quit thinking like that, but I know she was in so much pain.

"I've kept that deflated balloon, and I've framed it. I can look at it and know she's in a better place and with God and out of pain. But that was her sign to me on her son's birthday. And I believe that song is my sister's song. Every time I hear it on the radio, I think it's her way of saying, 'Sis, I'm okay.'"

"I love hearing that story," Aunt Jan says.

"There has to be something beyond this Earth!" Aunt Susie exclaims. She turns to her daughter Olivia. "Liv, that story makes me think of what happened to *us* a while back."

"What happened?" I ask.

Susie says, "About two or three years after your mom passed, Liv and I had been doing some shopping, and we were driving home. Sister Sledge's song 'We Are Family' came on the radio. There was a car in front of us, and the license plate said 'ANN 1122'!"

I feel the hair on the back of my neck stand up. This is the first time I've heard this story.

Susie smiles at me. "November 22 is your birthday. . . correct?"

I nod, shocked.

Susie continues with the story, "Minutes later we get behind this other car, and the license plate says 'CORKY'!"

There's a chorus of animated reactions: "What?!" "Nooooo!" "Really?"

Aunt Patty states, "It is a lot like the story about Corky and his keys. Do you all remember what happened?"

Aunt Cindy excitedly says, "Yeah! When Cork was sick, he kept talking about those damn keys that unlocked his old business. We never could find them. Two days after he died, Seth sat back in his old recliner and BAM! There they were!"

"All this stuff is weird," I admit. "The academic in me finds it all hard to believe, but you have to wonder if the dead can contact us."

Aunt Cindy responds, "I truly believe they can, and—"

She's interrupted by the clinking of piano keys from the corner of the room. I follow several pairs of astonished eyes to a peculiar scene. Lying at the foot of the piano is a stuffed doll.

HOME

My grandmother looks at it over her shoulder in astonishment. "Did someone accidently knock that thing off the piano?"

An eerie silence engulfs the room. All the family members shake their heads no. Everyone looks at one another suspiciously, inquisitively, and with a glimmer of hope.

"It's like someone picked it up and threw it down on the keys!" I exclaim.

My heart almost jumps out of my chest when I realize that I was mistaken about the object being a doll.

It was a stuffed snowman.

* * *

Six months later, as I'm running back in DuQuoin again, each foot quickly pounding the gravel road, I reflect on the events of the holiday season. I wonder whether the "signs" my family and I encountered of my mother were actually her communicating with us. Through the middle of town, on a literal jog down memory lane, I see and feel Mom everywhere.

I pass the town's elementary and middle school. This was the site of many of my band and chorus concerts my mother would attend. I also remember how every morning before school she would try to embarrass me. When dropping me off in front of the school, she would turn the music on the radio up to full blast.

I continue my run and begin to head down Main Street. I pass my Grandma and Grandpa Strong's old house. This was the site where the madness of having a family of nine manifested. Memories flash through my mind: practicing for piano lessons on their grand piano in the living room; favorite Christmases spent sitting in the dining room and listening to everyone chatter while enjoying the iced sugar cookies my grandmother ordered from the local bakery; coming by after church on Sunday mornings drinking Coke and eating Kit Kat bars while the Strong women chattered about their lives; and Easters spent looking for plastic eggs filled with money. My grandparents had to start using slips of paper with amounts of money written on them because a few of the eggs were misplaced one year.

I think about how holidays aren't the same as they used to be, and I have no idea who currently lives in the home or what it looks like on the inside.

I spot Mrs. Thompson's house in the distance. I used to take piano lessons from her. She was a cheerful middle-aged woman who was always optimistic about my musical skills even when I didn't practice nearly enough as I should have. She gave me free lessons after my mother died. "It's the least I can do," she said.

DuQuoin's famous Grand Theater still stands on Main Street. It's so old that I remember my grandmother telling me a story about how the owner constructed a pretend yellow-brick road outside the entrance for the opening of *The Wizard of Oz*. This is the only theater I can remember where you could see an evening show for a few dollars. People would joke about your feet sticking to the dirty floors. Some of the chairs were half broken, and occasionally a film would be canceled because the projector broke. Mom would take my brother and me to see a flick on Friday nights after a long day of doing hair. I particularly remember when James Cameron's *Titanic* played in theaters and her putting her hands over both of our eyes during the scene where Jack paints a nude portrait of his girlfriend Rose. I guess Mom figured we weren't ready to see Kate Winslet's breasts.

I pass the Catholic church where my mother's funeral was held. I imagine the line of people who stood about a mile down the street waiting to pay their respects to our family. I also try to think of happier moments in this former place of worship. I remember going to the Christmas Eve candlelight vigil service. A pleasing vision of Mom wrapping her arm around me with our faces glowing in the darkness as we sang "Silent Night" makes me smile.

I pass the Zimmerman's large two-story brick home, and I can see their underground pool in the backyard. Every Fourth of July they would host a barbeque. My family would go nearly every year. When I was really young and still had a fascination with magic, I thought the fireworks were fairies. Mom would get embarrassed when I repeatedly yelled, "Wheeee! Mom! Look at the fairies! Wheeee!" One year I almost drowned in the deep end of the pool. Mr. Zimmerman jumped in and pulled me to the surface. I remember this was one of the times I had seen my mother afraid. She had tightly grabbed my arm and shook me, saying, "You scared the shit out of me! Don't you ever do that again!" Then she hugged me and started to cry.

I know what this fear is like—watching someone potentially be torn from your life forever.

I'm relieved to see the sign for my family's street in the distance, Seminole Drive. My run around town is almost over. Ironically, Eric Church's

HOME

"Give Me Back My Hometown" comes on my iPod. Church's character in the song is telling a story about losing someone. But the character refuses to let the pain of the loss taint his memories of his hometown. For me, re-membering Mom on this run helps me enhance the memories of my hometown.

I don't ask anyone to give me back my hometown.

I reclaim it all on my own—one memory and one mile at a time.

* * *

"I like how it reads that she needs to cook Cindy's" Aunt Patty says as she points to a framed page of my mother's appointment book.

It's a Sunday afternoon, and all of my mother's sisters (Janet, Cindy, Patty, and Susie) have enthusiastically agreed to engage in a re-member-ing process about Mom. They're all sitting on an extra large sofa in the living room at Aunt Cindy's house. On the coffee table in front of them are several items: a photo from my junior prom in which Mom is helping me fasten my bow tie on the tuxedo; an April angel ceramic figurine that was a gift from Mom to Aunt Cindy; an album of pictures from Mom's fortieth birthday celebration cruise with her friends to the Bahamas; Mom and Dad's wedding album; and a framed page of Mom's appoint-ment book. In front of this page is a 5-by-7 picture of Mom, Aunt Cindy, and Uncle John at a Christmas celebration. "Look at their mischievous smiles," Aunt Cindy observes. "It looks like they are up to no good."

I fiddle with my new video recorder as they look through the memen-tos. As I focus in on them reviewing the artifacts, I feel as if there are four pieces of Mom in front of me. All Strong sisters sport the same dark brown hair color and have vibrant personalities. At family get-togethers, they tend to speak loudly and all at once. Today is no exception. They look through the mementos with excitement and do what Mom used to refer to as "hyena laughing" every few minutes.

My Aunt Jan is the eldest of the Strong sisters. Cindy, Patty, and Susie follow her in age. All of them, except Susie, use their reading glasses to get a better look at the artifacts. I laugh after watching Aunt Jan review an album and then look up and almost smack faces with Aunt Patty, who's also leaning in. Patty jumps back and laughs. She then reaches out and pretends that she's going to sexually grope Jan. "Woo woo, sexy!" she yells. It wouldn't be a Strong family event without their antics. My mother's comedic abilities live on through these women.

87

The women turn to my parents' wedding album and point and make various observations, each contributing to one another's memory. "Now how old was Ann when she got married?" Patty asks.

"Eighteen years old," I respond.

"I thought so!" my Aunt Jan adds.

After about forty-five minutes of reviewing the pictures, I say, "The first few questions are in the same format. So I'll ask, 'Tell me a story about Ann' as. . . and then I'll finish with some aspect of her identity. For example, the first question is 'Could you tell me a story about Ann as a young girl?'"

The sisters begin sharing their experiences, and I find myself slipping back in time, to even before I was just a gleam in my mother's eye. I start to develop a picture of who Ann Paxton was as a sister. . .

Ann was a rather large baby, ten pounds and ten ounces. The three older sisters (Patty, Cindy, and Jan) remember Grandma bringing her home from the hospital. "She had that one lazy eye," Patty remembers. It was one physical characteristic that stayed throughout her life.

My Aunt Susie was thirteen months younger than Mom. Growing up, they shared a room and bed. Susie remembers them playing all day outside in the summertime. When Mom was eleven, she had a bad fall on her ten-speed bike that left scars on her thighs. Susie also remembers them both being left in the care of several babysitters, including a seventy-something-year-old woman named Vergie who used to make them watch her soap opera, The Edge of Night.

The other sisters also have memories of Ann (or Annie Lou or Lou Lou Belle). They remember her having a lisp and talking about her kindergarten teacher Mrs. Bullock, which she would pronounce Mrs. Boo-lock. Susie and Annie were known as "the Grimers" because they were always caught eating sticky candies. Aunt Jan remembers Mom and Susie in their shorts eating licorice and suckers and Lik-M-Aids. Mom was a lot taller and chubbier than Susie, something she joked about throughout her life. Some family members gave them the nicknames Pebbles and Bam Bam, based on the Flintstone characters.

Aunt Cindy shares one especially humorous story of Mom as a child. Grandma used to take Annie and Susie out to Cindy's house to get their haircuts. Cindy and her husband, John, owned livestock. One day Cindy was out on the back patio cutting Susie's hair when Mom decided to get on top of a dirt pile and moo at the cows. Susie turned to laugh at Mom, and Cindy accidentally cut her hair too short. A month later, they were on a vacation and Susie held the door for two elderly ladies and they responded, "Thank you, sonny!" This is where Susie's nickname "Butch" came from.

HOME

Susie and Mom got along well. Susie rarely remembers any feelings of competition or fighting between them, even though many of her friends came over to their house to see not only her but also Mom. A few of Susie's friends were on the dance team with Mom, and she fondly remembers them telling her about a time Mom impersonated Brooke Shields during one practice. There was a 1980 Calvin Klein jean commercial in which Shields pulled on a pair of tight jeans and seductively contorted herself on the floor. The girls laughed as Mom rolled up her shirt and tossed and turned on the gym floor, screaming, "Look at me! I'm Brooke Shields in my sexy Calvins!"

That Strong sense of humor carried on into her life as a young wife and mother. Patty laughs as she describes Mom's wild driving and how she'd get nervous about her daughter Kirsten getting rides from her. "I was an overprotective mother, and I always made sure Kirsten wore her seat belt," Patty explains. "But your mom would pick her up in the old red Pontiac Grand Am she used to have. She'd say, 'Oh, forget the damn seatbelt. This ain't like your mom's driving! You're with the fun aunt now.' Your mom drove fast. It made me so damn nervous."

This tale inspires my Aunt Cindy to talk about a time Mom was pulled over in town by a police officer, one of her friend's husbands. Cindy can barely tell the story without laughing: "We're on our way home from a shopping trip, and all of a sudden we hear WOO WOO! Donny Baer, the officer, gets out of the car. Ann says, 'What the hell do you want, Baer?' He responds by telling her that her license plate sticker is expired. Your mom digs through her glove compartment and pulls out the updated sticker and says, 'Fuck you, Baer. It's right here. I haven't had time to put it on.' Mom gets out of the car, puts the new sticker on, and drives away without getting a ticket—a memorable end to a shopping trip.

The sisters shared a lot of time shopping together, and they tried to meet for Christmas shopping every year. Aunt Jan remembers once when there was a horrible snow and ice storm. "But your mom was bound and determined to go. She said, 'I've been saving for months for this!' We're sliding around on the interstate and we see several cars in the ditch. It was crazy!"

Since Aunt Cindy and my mother both had Mondays off, they had the most shopping experiences together. Sometimes they were stuck taking me with them. Aunt Cindy says, "One time—you were probably about seven or eight years old— you threw a fit when your mom wouldn't get a book you wanted because it was too expensive. We stopped by the Sonic drive-thru on the way home, and she tried to make things better by offering you ice cream. You pouted, crossed your arms, and said that you didn't want anything. Your mom responded, 'Good! There will be more ice cream for us!'"

Not only do the sisters have a lot of memories of Mom as a "tough love" type of mother, but also they're bursting with stories of her as a hairdresser. Every niece and nephew were used as guinea pigs for the newest hairstyles. Aunt Patty describes several times when Mom had to "fly by the seat of her pants." All the sisters say that Mom was a "damn good hairdresser" but was very disorganized. Sometimes she'd run out of gloves to put hair color on, so she'd use ziplock bags instead. One day she ran out of permanent solution and had to go borrow a bottle from another hairdresser. She had to use a lint roller to get excess dog hair off the chairs. Instead of a booster seat for young kids, she would stack books and magazines on top of each other. She used to not change her barbicide as often as she should, so instead of it being its normal dark blue color it was sometimes a milky white. Despite all these mishaps, business always boomed for Mom, and some nights she would work until nine o'clock.

The sisters appreciate one special thing Mom did as a hairdresser. After their father died, Mom made sure she went to the funeral and styled and colored his hair like she always had when he was alive. "He looked very nice," Aunt Susie says softly. "We'll never forget the great things she did for us."

"Look! There's a butterfly outside the front window!" Aunt Patty exclaims.

Aunt Cindy responds, "Oh yes! There are always two playing with each other there by my flowers. But it's odd—every time I talk about your mom, it always seems like there's a butterfly around. One time I was telling a story about Ann to one of the grandbabies in the backyard, and a butterfly sat right on my fingertip!"

"I keep hearing about people connecting spirits to butterflies. What is the meaning behind that?" I ask.

Aunt Jan states, "I think they have to do with new beginnings. You know, the butterfly was once a caterpillar..."

"Yeah! Like it's about metamorphosis," Aunt Patty adds.

Our discussion of the mystical creature is interrupted by Aunt Cindy's cell phone ringing from the kitchen. "I've got to answer. I think it might be Ryan," Aunt Cindy says and goes to fetch her phone. Ryan is her eldest son, who just got married and is traveling on his honeymoon. Due to inclement weather, there have been a few delays, and Cindy has been a little worried about their vacation plans.

"I'm going to go pour myself a glass of tea," Patty says and follows Cindy into the kitchen. Aunt Jan pulls out her cell phone and checks her text messages. Susie stares out the window. It appears there's something on her mind.

"Are you okay?" I ask.

She looks at me with deep sadness. When I stare into her eyes, I can feel her urgent yearning for the presence of her closest sister again. "I just miss her. In some ways, I think God prepared me for her death when Kenny took his job and moved." About three years before my mother died, my Uncle Kenny took a job in a town three hours north of DuQuoin, and he and his wife, Susie, and their two girls moved and started a new life. Susie has confided in me before that she hated not being able to be around as much when Mom struggled with her illness.

"It's like God prepared me for her future absence," she adds.

When Cindy and Patty return, and everyone settles back on the sofa, I finish the interview with a few questions.

"What has Mom's death taught you about being a sister?"

I ask this question for another purpose besides this project. Most of the sisters get along with one another, but there has always been a tension between Cindy and Patty.

In this moment, by asking this question about sisterhood, I wonder whether some relational improvement might begin.

The sisters spend a few moments in uncomfortable silence.

"As a sister?" Aunt Jan asks. I nod.

Aunt Cindy responds, "Your mom was the glue that held us together."

Aunt Patty's eyes widen in surprise. "You stole the words out of my mouth. I was getting ready to say that!"

Susie adds, "We used to get together a lot more."

Cindy nods enthusiastically. "She was easygoing and funny, even if some of her jokes were made at her own expense. She was the family peacekeeper, and she was the one who kept everybody together. I try to have holidays and get-togethers at the house, but your mom was always the one to initiate these things. I love her, and I miss her. They say if you touch one person in this life, you've done your job. She touched everybody."

Aunt Jan smiles. "They say only the good die young!"

* * *

I wander aimlessly around the hospital corridors, clutching a building map in my hand. The MapQuest application intones from my shorts' pocket, "Recalculating. Recalculating. . ." *Shut the hell up.* I turn off the application and force myself to stop pacing. *4:18 p.m. You can still make your 4:30 appointment with Dr. Grayson. You just have to quit being stubborn and ask someone to help you find his office.* I spot a nurse taking a drink from a water fountain.

"Excuse me. Could you tell me how to get to McGanon 435?" I ask and present her the building map—as if she's unfamiliar with the hospital.

"Go all the way down this hall and make a left. That's where you will find the elevators. Take one up to the fourth floor. I'm not sure after that, but you'll have signs to direct you."

As I walk to the elevator, I feel sweat rolling down my forehead. Even though the hospital is cold, my nerves cause me to sweat profusely. I've never interviewed a doctor before—let alone my mother's doctor and a neurosurgeon. I take the elevator to the fourth floor, and the voices of family members resound in my psyche.

"That Dr. Grayson. . . what a prince of a man!"

"He was the best doctor. He did so much for your mother."

"That guy is one of the best neurosurgeons in the country. You have to wait two years to see him, even with a referral from another doctor."

I always prepare interview questions, but for this occasion I've taken extra precautions. A few nights before, I tried to read everything I could find on my mother's illness. I also called one of my best friends, who's in medical school, to review my questions. I didn't want to sound like an idiot.

Following the signs to "Department of Neurosurgery," I find a waiting room with a couch and two plush armchairs. There's an empty desk to my left and a glass door on my right. At the desk, I spot a phone next to a laminated list of names and phone numbers. Scanning the list, I fail to see Grayson's name. Uncertain about how to proceed, I decide to take a seat on the sofa and wait to see if someone will approach the desk.

A man in a white lab coat walks up to the desk and looks down at a file folder. "Hey, Sam!" he yells. "Do you have anything on this Baxter case? They're coming in for a follow-up in the morning." He picks up the folder. As he walks to the other corner of the room, where I assume Sam must be, he glances at me and then buries his gaze in the folder. *Well, he was helpful.* Since the man isn't proving to be of much assistance, I decide to venture through the glass door on my right. But before I do,

92

HOME

a woman in a black pantsuit walks into the waiting room. "Can I help you, sir?"

"Yes," I say as I clumsily drop my notes. The woman helps me gather them up. "I have a four-thirty appointment with Dr. Grayson." She takes my name and asks me to have a seat. After a few minutes, she returns and notifies me that Grayson is ready.

With every step I take, my heart beats faster. This is the most anxious I've ever been about an interview.

I'm surprised to find that Grayson's office is much like a university faculty member's office. A large desk with stacks of papers and folders is in front of me. A desktop computer sits off to the side. I spot a bookcase in the corner of the room. One of the books, Eben Alexander's *Proof of Heaven: A Neurosurgeon's Journey into the Afterlife*, catches my eye. I've heard about this book, but I've never read it. Seeing it gives me some relief because it suggests that Grayson is spiritual.

His appearance doesn't surprise me, because I've already looked up his profile online numerous times in the past ten years. Grayson's white lab coat is draped around his desk chair, and he wears black slacks and a light blue dress shirt. I try not to giggle when I think about my mother saying, "He's pretty easy on the eyes, that Dr. Grayson."

He shakes my hand. "It is nice to meet you, Blake." His handshake feels smooth and cold, symbolic of a surgeon's aggressive scalpel.

"It's nice to finally meet you! I have heard many great things," I respond.

"Please take a seat." He gestures to the chair in front of his desk.

Before I sit down, I take out my recorder. "Is it okay if I record this interview?"

"Sure."

We go through normal introductory remarks, and then I get to my first question. "I have heard from various family members about the nature of my mother's condition. I have my own memories from ten years ago, but it would be nice to hear about the diagnosis from you."

"Sure." He turns to his computer. "I have her complete medical records here and. . ."

As he speaks, I find myself getting lost in the medical discourse. *Pituitary adenoma, pituitary carcinoma, ACTH, Cushing's disease, Cushing's syndrome, cavernous sinus, metastasize, carotid artery, gamma knife radiation.*

The terms make me dizzy. They're found in patients' charts and medical textbooks. In an attempt to feel closer to my mother in this moment, I wrap myself in cold hard facts. Even though I've just had information thrown at me, I'm able to take thorough notes and assemble a summary of my mother's condition:

> My mother was diagnosed with a pituitary adenoma. Dr. Grayson informs me that these are common, maybe as many as 20 percent of adults have them. My mother's tumor was large and invaded the cavernous sinus, which contains several nerves and a carotid artery that supplies blood to the brain. My mother's tumor secreted a hormone called ACTH that causes the adrenal glands to produce excessive amounts of cortisol, a steroid hormone. This results in Cushing's Disease, which is when the symptoms my mother experienced (weight gain, excessive facial hair, water retention, moon face, hump back) are often accompanied by a tumor.

Since my mother's tumor was so close to many important nerves, including some that control eye movement, Dr. Grayson was not able to completely remove it. After removing what they could, he and his team submitted it to the pathologist for further testing. The World Health Organization ranks the grade of these tumors on a scale of one to four, as far as how quickly they grow. My mother's tumor was a number two atypical pituitary adenoma, which signified future steady growth of the tumor. Gamma knife radiation was used to slow the growth of the tumor, and her adrenal glands were removed. Unfortunately, my mother's tumor metastasized to the other parts of her body, and this resulted in pituitary carcinoma.

"How rare is this?" I ask.

"In my twenty years in this department, my colleagues and I have only seen five patients, including your mother, with it."

"And of those cases, has anyone survived?

"We have one woman who has been doing a combination of radiation and chemotherapy for years. It has been a painful experience for her."

"Dr. Grayson, this is something I have wondered for a long time. You hate to think of a family member still alive but blind. If you had completely removed the tumor, could my mother have been alive but blind?"

"Even if we had removed the tumor, not only would your mother's vision be at risk, but we could have hit one of the main arteries that supplies blood to the brain, resulting in paralysis or death."

HOME

This makes me feel somewhat relieved. I would not have known this had I not taken the time to meet with Dr. Grayson. I conclude the interview with a few questions about what he thinks is the biggest obstacle to patient and doctor communication and his philosophy of patient care. "I have seen hundreds of patients, but your mother was very memorable," he says.

"Oh? Why is that?" If I'm honest with myself, I know I'm asking this because I want to see if he can give me an answer that relates to something other than the rarity of her case. Something personal.

"She had a wonderful attitude. . . very optimistic. Many people faced with her condition tend to want to give up. Your mom was a fighter."

Yes, and this ruined the quality of the end of her life.

Grayson asks about my father.

"He is doing well and is remarried. He speaks so highly of you, and he appreciated you leaving a message on our answering machine when Mom died."

"Like I said, your mom was a special patient. I'm sorry things didn't work out."

"I am too. But I don't think I'd be doing this research had I not had this experience. I guess if there's a silver lining, this would be it."

"True. I understand your need for doing this research. When my father died two years ago, I was doing medical research in Africa, and I remember just wanting his doctor to send everything to me. I needed to assess the situation for myself."

Dr. Grayson's pager interrupts our conversation. Within seconds his office phone rings, and I take it as a signal to end the interview.

I smile. "You are a busy guy. I appreciate you giving up some of your time. Thank you."

"You're welcome. Let me know if there is anything else I can do," he responds as we walk out of his office.

On my drive home, I try to process our interview. Dr. Grayson is an outstanding, personable doctor. He answered all of my questions and devoted nearly an hour of his day to speaking with me. But for some reason, it feels like something is missing—as though I was expecting more from the interview. *Did I expect him to cry as he spoke of her? Or for us to have a warm emotional moment in which he told me a personal story about her? Or that we would share a hug?*

I guess those sorts of experiences only happen in movies.

"It does fucking suck what you went through, Mom," I say out loud.

95

I turn on the radio and am pleased to hear a familiar country song, Justin Moore's "If Heaven Wasn't So Far Away." I turn it up and begin singing along. *Heaven is far away, but you are not, Mom. Although our relationship may be different now, it is still alive, and I can reconnect with you every day. I'm sorry it has taken me so long to figure this out.*

* * *

I stare at the plastic storage box that I just found underneath my parents' bed. It's thickly coated in dust, and when I pull it open I cringe at the gray smudges that are left on my fingers. I dust my hands off on my jeans and peer inside. I begin to sift through items that represent my mother's last years of life.

I go through the funeral guest book. In this particular book, there isn't any space for personal messages, but it's nice to see the many names of close friends written on each line. There are close to a hundred sympathy cards. The senders' words of support bring me comfort even ten years after Mom's death. "I am devastated." "Our thoughts and prayers are with you." "She was a special lady." "We will miss her so much." "I know she's up there laughing and doing hair." I smile at the last comment. One interpretation of Heaven I once heard is that whatever you enjoy doing the most in life, you'll be doing there. I know Mom's two favorite activities were doing hair and being a mother.

I find a list of chores on a scrap piece of paper scrawled in my mother's messy handwriting. I glance at a few of the tasks: fix button on Lindon's shirt; sign Kyle up for flag football; mop kitchen floor; pick up Blake's allergy medicine. A simple list of quotidian tasks can make me feel connected to her. I envision her dancing to a country music song as she mops the kitchen floor. I'm sure she also was having a conversation with Maddie, our family dog.

A flashy purple unopened envelope catches my eye. On the front I recognize my handwriting, and I've addressed this card to Dad. In the top left corner, my father has written "2-14-05, First Valentine's Day Without Ann." I open the envelope and find a Valentine's Day card I had given to him. Why would I have thought it would be a good idea to do this? Why would Dad choose to never open it?

I shake these questions off and move to the next item, a newspaper clipping that reads: "In loving memory of Ann Paxton, who passed away two years ago, December 19, 2004. Gone, but not forgotten. Absent, but always near. How we missed the presence Of the one we loved so dear." I'm not sure why the "Of" is capitalized. A typo, perhaps?

I find Kyle's poem he wrote and read at the funeral. I pick up the yellow notebook paper and read it to myself: "Mom is great. Mom is fun. I was her son. I guess her time had come but her new life has just begun. Mom's pain is over, gone, done. Now, she is my guardian angel, shining like the sun." This was so touching during her funeral, and it was a big achievement for my brother. He has a difficult time expressing his feelings. I'm even more touched to see that every "is" in the poem was written above a crossed-out "was."

Aside from the personal items, I notice more clinical mementos. I rummage through them and find my mother's death certificate. "Cause of death—pulmonary embolism," it reads. Additionally, there are discharge papers, a hospital guidebook, copies of prescriptions, and one of Mom's driver's licenses. At first, I don't understand why Dad would want to hold on to these things—detached reminders of the most painful aspects of my mother's life. But I can understand that this information might be useful should I ever need to know my family's medical history.

Next, I see a white hardbound book. I turn it over and find that the cover is a cartoon of a baby in a bassinet surrounded by an angel and various creatures: birds, lambs, rabbits, and puppy dogs. Opening it, I'm pleasantly surprised to discover that it's my baby memory book. The first page has a picture of an angel blowing a horn, and underneath is a message that reads:

That Special Day
November 22, 1986 (Baby's Birthday)
This is the day which the lord hath made, we will rejoice and be glad
   in it

(Ps:118:24).

The second page contains information about my birth. I had no idea that people kept track of this stuff: first indications Mom was going into labor; when she arrived at the hospital; my full name, weight, length, hair color, eye color, doctor, pediatrician, and nurses. I look through the rest of the book and find other items: a door deck in the shape of a green kangaroo with my name on it; the bracelet I wore in the hospital; a cigar for Dad; and a picture of me in my mother's arms just after she delivered me, my skin inflamed and covered with placenta fluid.

"You were quite the aggressive baby when I delivered you," my mother used to say. "Your brother, on the other hand, moved at a snail's pace. I always joke and say that you ended up acting opposite when you were toddlers—you being calm and easygoing, and your brother being hyper and always causing a ruckus."

I place the baby book back in the container. *Okay. I think this is good enough.* When I begin to close the box, I notice a bright red paper booklet with the title "DHS Class of '82: Celebrating 20 Years" in bold black letters. This must be the program from my mother's twenty-year high school reunion. I read through a few of her classmates' listings, and then I get to Mom's entry:

> Spouse's Name: Lindon Paxton
>
> Children: Blake (15 years old) Kyle (11 years old)
>
> Education: 1 year of Cosmetology at John A. Logan Community College
>
> Current Employment: Hairdresser at home

Plans for the future:

> Continue to work as a hairdresser for the next 20 years and enjoy watching my boys grow up.

* * *

"Sometimes you don't realize how the smallest thing can mean so much to someone. I didn't know until six months before your mom died how much that moment in high school meant to her," Sarah Morgan says.

It's the middle of the afternoon, on a Wednesday. Sarah and I sit at her dining room table. "That was a powerful story, Sarah," I say. I dig out tissues from my pocket and hand them to her. "Thank you for doing that for Mom."

Sarah had been a client and friend of my mother's. She told me a story from their high school days. When my mother was a sophomore in high school, she had to take a physical education (PE) class with girls two years older than her. "The first day of class, I remember seeing your mom sitting in the bleachers all by herself," Sarah told me. "The second day, I introduced myself. We were friends from that moment."

Her story, even in its simplicity, moves me deeply. I picture a young Ann, insecure and scared as hell and wondering if she'll have any friends in that PE class. Then I see Sarah, with her bright and bubbly persona, melting all of my mother's fears away. I don't know why this simple act of kindness means so much to me. Maybe it's because I know what it's like to constantly worry about fitting in with peers. Maybe it's because there were times I'd felt alone and isolated from others, times I needed someone like Sarah in my life.

"Can you tell me what you remember about Mom as a mother?" I ask.

Sarah chuckles as she dabs tears. "Do you remember you and Claire used to go to nursery school together?"

I nod. Claire is Sarah's daughter, and she and I are the same age.

"Your mom and I would take turns dropping off and picking you up from school. The school used to get book order packets every couple of weeks. And you loved to read as a kid, and you'd always want to order books, every time. So. . ." She laughs. "I'd drop you off at your house, and your mom would be working, and you'd walk in with those book order packets, and she'd stand there and yell, 'Another fucking book order! Are you kidding me? I just got him books two weeks ago!'"

It seems that with every interview I keep hearing about my mother's abundant use of the F-word. Memories of this, and the way she used to refer to her large breasts as "cow titties," make me laugh.

Sarah continues, "But I never heard you say that word as a kid, even though your mom said it in front of you all the time. Your mom had her own unique style of mothering. She wasn't really affectionate with you and your brother, but you knew that she cared about you so much. You boys were her world. It didn't matter if she'd been working a ten- or twelve-hour day—if Kyle had a sporting event or you had a music concert, she was there. She was a special mother and a special person. God, I miss her."

"What do you remember about her during her time of illness?"

"I don't know if you knew this," she says, "but I had a pituitary tumor, too."

"What? I don't think anyone has told me that."

Sarah looks just as surprised as I am that I don't know this information. "We would often compare notes about our experiences and symptoms."

"Did you have surgery for yours?"

"No. I did not have Cushing's disease like your mother, because instead of producing ACTH my tumor produced a hormone called prolactin. My physician still monitors it to this day, and I have to take medicine to regulate it and keep it from growing."

"That's good it can be regulated."

Sarah sighs deeply. She doesn't seem relieved by this information, and she shifts in her seat uncomfortably. "I've had a lot of guilt about why God took your mother and left me. I feel like she had a lot more to give."

Her voices quivers, and I can see the years of pain radiating from her eyes. "She loved life so much, and I don't understand how you can have two people around the same age with the same location of tumor but they were able to fix me. . . and not her."

I walk over to her side of the table and give her a sideways hug, placing my cheek on the top of her head. This moment is strangely intimate. Until this day, aside from occasional emails, I had barely spoken to Sarah. But her disclosure of disease has brought me closer to her—and to Mom.

"But Sarah, you do have so much to give. My mother would not want you to feel this guilt," I reassure her.

"Thank you. But your mother touched lives positively everywhere she went. It's hard remembering her when she was sick. There was one day. . . I don't know if you want to hear this." She looks at me and searches my face, looking for permission to tell her story.

I give her a tight squeeze and return to my seat. "Yeah, go ahead."

"Do you remember that some of her friends and clients took turns taking her to the doctor when your family members couldn't?"

"Yes."

"One day we were returning from her endocrinologist and she says: 'Sarah, I have to talk to you about something. I need to talk to somebody, and nobody wants to talk about it.' And of course I said, 'Annie, you just talk, babe.' She said, 'I know that I'm going to die, and I want the boys to be prepared.'"

A chill rolls down my spine. I never heard from anyone that Mom thought about dying.

Sarah places her hand on my arm. "You okay, babe?"

"Yes. So she really thought she would die?"

"I tried to reassure her that we would beat this, but she wouldn't let up, so I let her talk. She told me she had put things away, like all of her

100

jewelry and certain papers. She was worried about leaving you and your brother behind and about what your Dad would do without her."

Many people don't want to think about a family member dying, but after hearing Sarah tell me this, I wonder if my mother's final months would've been easier for all of us had we considered the possibility. I'm grateful that Sarah provided an outlet for my mother and relieved some anxiety about what she knew might happen. I find it interesting that Sarah needs to talk about this information with me as much as my mother needed to talk to her about her possible death.

Sarah leans in and taps her hand on the table. "Another thing she talked about that day was how she thought you were gay."

I inhale. While I had heard that she had hinted to an aunt that she suspected I was gay, this was all I knew. For years, I've wondered how Mom would've reacted to me coming out. Now, knowing that I'll get some answers simultaneously enthralls me and paralyzes me with fear.

"Your mom said that if she were here when you decided to come out, she'd fight for you," Sarah says. "But she worried about how your father would take the news. I told her that he would come around. It may be a shock at first, but if you love your kids you'll accept it, and you realize they are the same person even if they're gay. I told your mom she should prepare your dad in case you decided to come out. So I guess she probably discussed it with him."

I shake my head back and forth. My mother never mentioned to my father that she thought I was gay. I remember four years ago when I told him. His response was, "Well, I'm not tickled pink about it." He never suspected I was gay, and he also was more disappointed that I had come out to other family members before coming out to him. At least I know that my mother would've been supportive.

There's a crinkle of frustration on Sarah's forehead. "I told her she should prepare him. But I guess things are all right with you and your father?"

"Yes. You were right. He has been pretty good about it. When he was in Tampa for my master's degree commencement ceremony, we went to Madeira Beach. This guy runs by without his shirt and Dad says, 'Hey, what do you think about that one?' I about pissed my pants. Not only was Dad validating that I was gay, but he was also suggesting a man was attractive!"

Sarah laughs. "Wow! Your dad is a great guy. He and your mom, though, they sure did fight hard, but we all knew they loved each other. I think sometimes the couples who love the hardest fight the hardest. You know?"

"I agree. My dad did so much for my mom. At one point, just to keep our insurance to pay for my mother's medical bills, he had to work three hours away from home. That's a six-hour commute!"

Sarah smiles and reaches over to touch my face. "They are both good people, and they brought up a wonderful young man. Your mom would be so proud of you."

I look down bashfully. "Thanks, Sarah."

"Anything else you need to ask me about?"

I review my notes and make sure the recorder is still going. "You've helped so much, Sarah. I'll close by asking if there is anything you'd like to say to conclude the interview."

Sarah takes a few moments to respond. As she begins to speak, she leans closer to the recorder, as if she wants to make sure this statement is completely captured. "It's remarkable that you've taken something that had to be such a tragedy and that you're turning it into something positive. Not only is it going to help give you peace, but it will help give your family peace, and all of your students and hopefully the rest of the world if they read your book. You can validate feelings, and you can change the way people view grief, and that's a gift. Your mother, she'll live on through your gift."

I click the stop button on the recorder. "Now that's a great ending!"

Sarah jumps up from the table with excitement. "Glad I can help. Now don't go anywhere—I have pot roast in the oven, and you're staying for dinner."

* * *

She'll live on through your gift.

Sarah's words swirl in my head as I drive home. I realize that she's right. For a long time, it was painful for me to return to DuQuoin. There were too many traumatic memories and too much fear of rejection. After being here for three weeks, I've realized that my fear was unnecessary. In almost every interview, an interviewee has asked me whether I've found a partner. None of them have pretended that my potential partner could be a woman, either. The more I've immersed myself in the field, the more I've reconnected with those

I left behind. The more I re-member Mom with others, the more I see this town with new eyes, and the more my pride in the community is restored.

As I pull into our driveway, I see my father sleeping in one of two folding chairs in front of the garage. Our family golden retriever, Sophie, sits between the chairs. I assume Dad has been mowing the lawn when I see small remnants of grass blades covering his arms. He sports an old gray T-shirt that says The Malt Shoppe—the name of the local restaurant he used to own—jogging shorts, and a worn pair of tennis shoes.

As I walk toward the chair next to him, Dad's eyes slowly open and a faint smile spreads across his face. "Hey, man. Why don't you turn that radio down?" Before sitting, I reach behind the chair and silence the Cardinal's baseball game broadcast.

It's almost sundown on this summer evening. The southern Illinois weather has been a nice change from the sticky, humid Tampa heat. A slight breeze threatens to blow my field notes away, so I place an empty red milk crate on them.

"How did your interview go?" Dad asks.

I reach out to pet Sophie. She recently received her spring haircut, and the fur is thick around her head and neck while the rest of the body is buzzed. "The interview went well. It is just hard for people to remember things about Mom. . . after more than ten years."

Dad scratches his thick gray beard, appearing deep in thought. "I hope all of these interviews can still be helpful."

"Of course!" I continue to pet Sophie. "You are such a pretty girl! Yes, so pretty. . ."

Dad lets out a chuckle. "She's my baby."

"Do you know Aunt Cindy doesn't know about her? How long have you had her?"

"Since Kelly and I got married . . . about six years."

"I guess it's still hard for her and the other sisters to come here. . ."

This house is where my mother died. In the few moments of strained silence, I continue to coo at the dog. Why can't I feel comfortable in this silence? Is it because I know that there's so much I want to say? Finally, I ask, "So can I interview you?"

"Yeah!" Dad says. "Why wouldn't you be able to?"

I shrug. "I don't know. I thought it might be difficult for you."

"Son, you can ask me anything."

Another moment of silence, and I notice the sun is beginning to set. The creatures of the night begin their chorus of various melodies: crickets chirping, an owl calling out, the faint sounds of a few neighborhood dogs barking. Even in the most residential areas of Tampa, this symphony of evening nature isn't quite as sweet to my ears as it is here in southern Illinois.

I think about what Sarah disclosed to me early in the afternoon, and I'm left wondering if Mom ever confided in Dad about the possibility of dying. Usually I'm too afraid to ask questions like these, but if I don't ask now, when will I ever?

"Did Mom ever talk to you about dying?"

My father's body stiffens as he looks off in the distance. He breathes deeply. "Not really. We tried to hope for the best. I do remember the last appointment we had with Dr. Grayson and the man who would have been her oncologist. It was on the Friday before she died that Sunday. Grayson showed us the X-ray of the brain and how the tumor was spinning out of control. He spoke with confidence, though. From what I remember, he suggested it would be difficult to manage, but it was possible.

"I never thought about her dying," he continues. "It seemed like every time you turned around, she was getting smacked in the face with something. The next night, on Saturday, we had gotten into an argument about your grandma. As always, your grandma wanted to run the damn show."

I vividly remember my Grandma Jo-Ann visiting when my mother was sick, and as soon as she could hear my father's truck grinding down the gravel road she would get up to leave. I've never been sure why there has been tension between the two of them, and my mother's illness seemed to make it worse.

"The next morning I went to mass. When I got home, she was still in bed. I crawled back under the blankets and held her. I kept telling her how sorry I was about the argument. . ." My father's voice quivers. "God, she just wasn't herself that day. Your Aunt Cindy called later in the morning, and we were talking about what we were going to do about Christmas gifts for you and your brother. Ann thought we were talking about her or something, and she got so angry. She started to scream, 'Quit acting like I'm fucking dying!' I had to settle her down before Father Jerome got there."

"Father Jerome came to the house?"

"Yes, he came and visited. He said some prayers. I think maybe that's what gave her anxiety because she felt like she was being given her last rites."

"Yeah."

"And then she started saying she felt really warm, and so I kept putting a washcloth on her face. She couldn't eat anything, had no appetite. Then, you came home, and you know the rest."

"Yes, I do. I've thought about that day a lot and have written about it. But it's always hard to think about, and I can remember the painful details. As time goes on, though, it's been easier to avoid thinking about it."

My father appears to be replaying that day in his mind. I feel some guilt for having him think about the day again. He turns to me and says, "But you know, there is one thing I still think about a lot since that day."

"What's that?"

"I often wonder if she loved me."

His statement is like a jab to the stomach. I quickly say, "Oh, Dad. I think she did."

Dad's eyes widen. "That's not something you should think. It's something you should *know*."

I'm embarrassed that I didn't say the right thing. I'm sure my father doesn't want to hear that there was hesitancy in my mother's love. I try to think of what else I can say. "Come on, Dad. She *did* love you. I *know* she did. What would make you think otherwise?"

My father's eyes slightly glisten. "I don't know. I just said things . . . teased her a lot."

"I am sure you both said things that you didn't mean. I always feel like people should be more concerned about couples who do not get into any disagreements than the ones who do. It is healthy to have some disagreements."

"If that's true, then our relationship was a great success."

"You both always stuck it out, though. To me that shows love." When I see that my statement isn't reassuring him, I get up from the chair and walk to him. "Come on, Dad. Get up."

I ease him out of the chair and hug him tightly. We stay like that for several minutes. I realize that I can only say so much.

Maybe I can take away some of the burden of this doubt that has plagued him for the last ten years and let him know that he was and is loved very much.

* * *

"Do we really have to record this?" Dad looks at the recorder like it's a venomous snake.

I sigh. "Dad, I need to record it because it will help me when I write up the interview. I can stop the recorder at any time. You'll barely even know it's here."

"All right," he says. It has been about three days since I spoke with Dad about my project. I've had to take a couple days off from the research because of the intensity of my grief. I've spent my time wisely, going for long jogs around town, catching up on my reading, and relaxing in Aunt Cindy's pool.

Dad and I are sitting in the living room. He's in his favorite armchair, and I'm on the brown leather sofa. The recorder is placed on the end table, the only thing physically separating us. I ask Dad if I can have a copy of Mom's death certificate that I found in the plastic container. As he rummages in his home office to find one, I scan the living room wall. A portrait of Dad and Kelly from their wedding day is mounted. Surrounding the photo, scrawled in black permanent marker, are messages from well-wishers. I'm glad Kelly is in our lives. She makes Dad happy.

Next to this portrait are two large frames housing a collage of photographs. Above them, painted in cursive, it says "Our Family." There are pictures of Kelly's four children and my brother and me at various parts of our lives, even before she and Dad were married. A few candid couple shots also are included. Although I appreciate Kelly's hard work in making this, I'm left wondering where my mother is in the collage. Isn't she still part of "our family?" I'm not angry with Kelly—just disappointed.

Dad comes back with a copy of the death certificate, and I shift my focus to our interview. He takes a few moments to settle into the chair, making sure to sit in the most comfortable position for his aching back. Every time I'm home I notice my father's aging process. I notice the little things—him limping to the fridge in the middle of the night for a glass of water, using reading glasses even though he's had LASIK surgery, and how his beard and the little hair he has left on his head continue to turn gray.

HOME

"Are you ready?" I ask.

"Go ahead."

I look at my notes. I feel peculiar interviewing my father. Although we've had some very intimate discussions, I'm wondering whether framing this discussion as an interview is going to have repercussions.

"Could you tell me a story about Mom as a young girl?"

A long moment passes. My father scratches his beard.

"What do you mean?" he asks.

Come on, Dad. It's not a hard question. I attempt to redirect. "What do you remember about her when she was younger? You've told me about how you two met. Maybe that's a good place to start."

Dad begins to narrate the story of his life with Mom. I'm able to see the relationship unfold. . .

Ann was more mature than a normal fourteen-year-old. I met her through your Uncle Joe, who was one of my best friends in school. When we were first dating, we spent a lot of time at your Grandma and Grandpa Strong's house playing pool in the basement, listening to music, and sneaking a beer from time to time.

Your Uncle Joe suggested I take your mom out for New Year's Eve. Your mom was a knockout. I was hesitant to ask her out, though. She was younger than me, and I had just been hurt by a former girlfriend. But, *I thought,* what the hell? *So, I asked her to the party. We went and had a good time. Damn nerves got the best of me on the way home. I told her that we probably wouldn't get serious because of the age difference. I think that upset her.*

We didn't talk for about a month. Then, I went to a basketball game with Joe. You remember your mom was on the school dance team? Halftime came around, and she came shimmying down the bleachers. I thought, You better get that girl back! *And so after the game, I apologized, and that's when it all started.*

I went with your mom to all her school dances. She used to cook meals for me and bring them over to me at my place. Mmm . . . She made the best meatloaf and mashed potatoes. Those potatoes were loaded with butter and salt. You remember?

Of course, I had a jealous streak. Every guy who talked to your mom I watched like a hawk. It got to be too much for her, and we took a break. That only lasted a couple weeks, though.

Your mom graduated that May, and we married in August. I don't remember how I asked her to marry me. We had a few conversations about marriage. One day, after going to the movies, we went and looked at rings. It was simple. We lived in a small one-bedroom apartment when we were first married. Your mom used to do people's hair there while she completed cosmetology school. After a couple years,

107

we decided to have this home built. Our first year in this house, we tried to get pregnant. It took us a while to get pregnant with you.

You were born on the Saturday before Thanksgiving. A high school football playoff game was also going on that day. Everybody was rushing back and forth from the hospital waiting room to the cars, trying to listen to the game. Ha! You were finally born after your mom was in eight hours of labor. But something wasn't right with your breathing... something hadn't developed fully. We had to transport you to another hospital thirty minutes away. But luckily, you ended up being okay, and we got to have you home for Thanksgiving.

The first few years raising you went pretty good. But then, after I got laid off at the coal mines, everything went to shit. Your mom had a miscarriage. She cried so much and could barely eat for weeks. When she went back to work, I decided to start a restaurant—the Malt Shoppe, I called it. Then, about a year after we opened, I was offered my job back at the mines. So I hired my co-manager Ken to help me work both jobs.

About two years after that, we had your brother. It was great watching you boys grow up. Your mom and I would go to his Little League games and your concerts and plays. She was able to go more than I was to those things. She would work a ten- or twelve-hour day of doing hair and then still turn around and go to one of you kids' events. My Annie, she was an amazing woman.

The beeping of the recorder interrupts my father's story. I realize I need to change its battery. "Hold on, Dad. I need to fix this. Sorry."

While I fidget with the recorder, Dad pours himself a glass of iced tea. Once we get situated again, I ask, "How would you describe your coping process after Mom's death?"

Dad continues his story...

In the first year after your mom was gone, she was constantly on my mind. I spent many nights at home wondering about a lot of things. Was there anything else I could have done? Could I have been a better husband? Could my words have been kinder in her final days?

I spent a lot of time talking to Father Jerome. In one conversation, I felt so guilty that I told him I thought I had killed your mom. I felt so bad and helpless. Of course, he told me that I did all I could do for her. He suggested maybe going to her grave and praying. So, for many weeks, I would do just that. I would have conversations with her while I was there . . . asking her for guidance. I can't think of a specific example, but I knew there were times where I felt like she responded to me.

There was this one specific dream I kept having about her, too. I would try to run after her, but I could never catch her. I took this as a message from her that I needed to move on with my life. So, it took me some time, but I started dating again. You remember I spent time with a couple women before I met Kelly.

I still miss her, but I know that I am blessed to have my health and family. I guess it's true that you don't know how good something is until it's gone.

I look down at my watch and am surprised to see that a full hour has passed. It's amazing that a span of eighteen years can be covered in this short amount of time. I ask the last question of the interview.

"If Mom could come back, just for a short period of time, what would you say to her?"

"I think the first thing I'd tell her was 'I love you. You never know how good you have it until it's gone. And thank you for letting me be a part of your life. I hope that I didn't wreck your life. Because it was a short one.'"

"You didn't, Dad."

"And. . ." Dad's voice quivers. "I'm so mad at you for going and leaving me."

"What would you hope that she would say?" I ask.

"I hope she would say she loved me."

I take my father's rough, callused hand in mine. "She would, Dad."

"And that her life was good."

"It was good, Dad. Before her illness, it was really good." I give his forearm a soft rub and turn the recorder off. "Thanks again, Dad. For doing this."

Dad flips on the television and starts channel surfing. We've said quite a bit to each other during the interview. I wonder whether this interview was helpful—for my father's coping process and for our relationship. Hopefully, this interview has started something special.

Through continuing a bond with Mom, I attempt to restore a bond with my father—that had for some time seemed somewhat strained.

CHAPTER 4

REASSESSING CONTINUING BONDS AND CHALLENGING THE CAUSALITY THESIS

Although much research has been completed on continuing bonds, many aspects of these relationships with the dead still need to be interrogated. Klass (2006) argues, "We do not yet know all the interactions that comprise what we now call continuing bonds. We are still developing a common set of terms with which to talk about them" (p. 857). In the remaining two chapters, I show how my narratives illuminate current understandings of continuing bonds but also help unearth different questions about them. I believe that communication researchers can make a strong contribution to the continuing bonds literature.

In this chapter, I summarize my observations about the complexity of continuing bonds and re-membering in my mother's community of grievers. I discuss how using certain communication theoretical frameworks (derived from research on family storytelling and end of life decision making) can assist future research about continuing bonds and re-membering scholarship. I demonstrate this through the ways in which people re-membered my mother—consistent with the current identified strategies in the literature but also differing in several instances. Although many experiences of re-membering during the research process were enjoyable, there were moments of discomfort. I address these experiences in the sections on the constraints and failures of continuing bonds and the emotional challenges in interactive interviews. My observations support Klass's resistance to what he coins the "causality thesis" in continuing bonds research.

Klass writes, "My work is often cited wrongly as claiming that continuing bonds support better adjustment. If I have ever implied such a thing, I apologize" (p. 844). Klass claims that when he and his colleagues developed the continuing bonds approach, it was not supposed to be interpreted as an antidote to loss. Rather, they developed this work to show that bonds with the deceased did not have to be deemed pathological. Klass states that scholars who have misused his and his colleagues' theory are promoting a "causality thesis"—the idea that continuing bonds cause healthy adjustment to a loss. The subsequent analyses of my field notes and interview transcripts show that, while continuing bonds may be emotionally powerful and rewarding for the bereaved, they do not always work well for everyone and should not be viewed as a panacea for the problems associated with mourning.

In order to build a case against the causality thesis, it is best to start with communication research that focuses on how families cope with a loved one's death or dying process. I show that a pragmatic approach to this research can help the bereaved grieve in the best way possible. The process of continuing bonds with the deceased will not "resolve" grieving, but rather help the bereaved embrace life and enrich their relationships with the living.

Re-Membering Stories of Post-Death Contact

Hedtke & Winslade (2004) have offered specific strategies, coined "re-membering" rituals, to aid families in a loved one's dying process and maintain relationships after death. According to their perspective, re-membering is not to be confused with simply reminiscing about the dead; instead, re-membering requires much more active, conscious processes in everyday life. Hedtke and Winslade argue that everyone we know is like a member in our club of life, and some members are more important than others (e.g., acquaintances versus close friends and family members). When someone dies, this does not mean that these individuals cease to be members in our club. Hence, we rely upon re-membering rituals to allow the deceased to regain active membership in our clubs. These rituals might include telling stories about those who have died, having imagined conversations with the deceased, celebrating their birthdays, memorializing the anniversaries of their deaths, and engaging with artifacts that represent or once belonged to them.

In continuing bonds research, scholars have described ways the bereaved can continue a relationship through more reflective and cognitive processes as well. These types of reflection processes include internalizing values and beliefs of the deceased (Klass, 1993); taking on personality traits of the deceased (Russac, Steighner, & Canto, 2002; Tyson-Rawson, 1996); participating in activities the deceased would have enjoyed (Foster et al., 2011); and recognizing the deceased as a role model for future behaviors (Marwit & Klass, 1996; Tyson-Rawson, 1996). Research has also shown how exploring possibilities of post-death contact (Kalish & Reynolds, 1976; Klugman, 2006) and the recognition of spiritual signs are also ways to continue a bond with and re-member the deceased (Rennels & Paxton, 2013; Valentine, 2008).

Many of these potential "signs" of the deceased may be described through family stories passed on from one generation to the next. The study of storytelling as a form of family ritual has been widely explored in communication studies, and a major part of continuing bonds or re-membering practices is through family storytelling. It is through storytelling that individuals "do family" (Langellier & Peterson, 2006) and interpret and explain experiences (Jorgenson & Bochner, 2004). In re-membering rituals, family members must decide when and what stories about the deceased are told. These stories construct the identity and memory of the deceased. They also construct the family's identity without the deceased's physical presence. As Attig (2001) argues, after a loss individuals must relearn their world without the loved one. Family storytelling rituals can help facilitate this relearning process.

There are common rituals for memorializing the dead. One common ritual for memorializing the deceased is visiting a family member's grave. There are certain tasks that are required for this particular activity—such as leaving flowers or mementos, praying and/or talking to the dead, or giving a moment of silence. Ellis (2003) has written about the mixed feelings people may have while performing these tasks. These contradictory feelings may result because of ideologies of moving on, and continuing bonds practices may be viewed as a sign of complicated grief. Concepts of closure and moving on might discourage family members from participating in these activities (e.g., visiting a grave), and this results in a lack of performance guidelines (what one should do or say while visiting a grave). Closure and "moving on" also affect the voluntary aspects of rituals, because people may want to participate in re-membering practices but fear stigmatization from other family members.

This stigmatization can affect the social nature of ritual. In terms of continuing bonds, individuals may have difficulty finding other family members to participate in the rituals because they fear rejection, others thinking they are mentally ill, or dwelling in the loss. Since we often conceptualize an individual's personhood in terms of physical presence, many may not realize that a deceased family member can still be the "passive enactment of the 'audience' role" (Baxter & Braithwaite, 2006, p. 261). By not talking about the deceased or not participating in rituals that reaffirm their personhood, individuals not only diminish the possibility of social relations with the deceased, but also suggest they do not value the lives they lived and the legacies they left behind. Hedtke and Winslade describe this as "dis-membering" the deceased (2004, p. 12). A funeral is a one-time event, but for some individuals, in order to fully reinstate the deceased's personhood, re-membering rituals need to occur regularly.

Within these types of rituals, many other phenomena occur. Baxter & Braithwaite (2006) argue that family rituals are condensed. Not only are family members continuing a relationship with the deceased, but also they may be determining how that person's legacy will continue. They may be taking care of unfinished business or resolving family disagreements surrounding the death. Through continuing bonds with the deceased, family members can discuss with one another how they want to be remembered after death. In order for these needs to be addressed, the re-membering ritual needs to be effective in fulfilling its foundational role of reconstructing a deceased family member's personhood. Spirituality and religion are two strong influences that can either constrain or encourage these types of re-membering family stories about the dead or possibilities of post-death contact.

In Keeley's (2004) work on final conversations among the terminally ill and their families, she found that spirituality and religion informed the coping processes for surviving family members. Survivors indicated that when final conversations focused around religion or spirituality, they often were prescribed certain behaviors or rules of conduct from the dying family members. One of the categories of rules of conduct was to "cope with life's challenges after a loved one is gone" (p. 93). Survivors indicated that terminally ill family members would request that they seek out their guidance in times of strife or look for signs of their presence after the death. It is highly probable that these final conversations with the terminally ill might inform the way families tell stories about them after they have died. Extending the parameters of Keeley's concept of "final conversations" to after a person has died may stimulate additional intriguing research questions about family storytelling and how stories about the deceased are jointly told among family members.

Koenig Kellas & Trees (2006) have demonstrated that specific sense-making behaviors occur when family members jointly tell stories about difficult experiences. In their work, they identified three different sense-making behaviors when family members jointly told stories: family-unit sense-making, individual family member sense-making, and in-complete sense-making. In family-unit sense-making, every family member is active in the telling of the story, and family members reach a shared conclusion about the experience. In individual family member sense-making, family members share with one another separate versions of a story and come up with their own meanings about the experience. Finally, in in-complete sense-making, one or more of the family members are not engaged in the telling of the story, and no clear meanings are deciphered. Koenig Kellas and Trees argue that this knowledge will help narrative and family therapists understand baseline behaviors of families before entering therapy.

As demonstrated thus far, it appears there was an instance of individual family member sense-making behaviors about stories of possible post-death contact from my mother. Aunt Cindy's story (as depicted in chapter 3) in which she discussed the possibility of my mother contacting her through a deflated balloon and song inspired other family members to give their versions of my mother contacting them. In retrospect, it appears that most of the family members present that day concluded these were actually messages from my mother. I do not know if some of the family members present denied the possibility of my mother contacting them through these experiences.

Additionally, the analysis of this experience on Christmas Day leaves me with several other questions: If all family members had been aware of Aunt Cindy's story, how would the sense-making behaviors have changed, and would this have implicated our family satisfaction and functioning? How would the sense-making behaviors for this story have been different if a family member present was either agnostic or atheist? Why were the men not as participatory in the sense-making process? How might my family jointly tell and make sense of Aunt Cindy's story and the story about that Christmas Day? Outside of my family, what factors would determine sense-making behaviors about stories with the specific topic of post-death contact?

Even if there is no tangible, physical evidence of afterlife communication, it is imperative that communication scholars consider how belief or disbelief in these experiences influences families. The ability to tell stories of post-death contact and continue a relationship with the deceased could be a major success for many families who are afraid to talk about a deceased loved one. The dead may not "really" give messages or respond to messages of the living, but this is not the point of studying these phenomena. As Peters (2001) observes:

> Our communication with the dead may never reach them, but such elliptical sending is as important as circular reciprocity. It would be foolish to disparage communications that never leave our own circle as only failures. That I cannot engage in dialogue with Plato or the Beatles does not demean the contact I have with them. Such contact may be hermeneutic and aesthetic rather than personal or mutual. I may have to supply all the replies they might make to my queries—rather like the contact I have with the universe. Or with myself.
>
> (p. 152)

There is much at stake if communication scholars do not consider the importance of these reported phenomena and how they can help people cope with grief.

Stories of post-death contact can help re-story family identities and enhance feelings of intimacy in the family system after occurrences of trauma and disruption. Every person will lose someone, and people grieve in different ways. Stories of post-death contact can do many things for bereaved families, but stories of post-death contact were not the only way my mother's community of grievers re-membered her. In the next section, I outline how the people I interviewed continued a bond with her, in ways both consistent with and different from currently identified strategies in the research about grief.

Specific Re-Membering Practices for Ann Paxton

As in every relationship, whether the other person is alive or dead, I found unique nuances in people's relationships with my mother. My interviewees expressed several ways they re-membered my mother and other deceased loved ones. Those ways were consistent with already established findings in the literature, including telling stories about and observing potential post-death contact, keeping items that belonged to or represented the deceased, participating in activities the deceased would have enjoyed, taking on personality traits of the deceased, and recognizing the deceased as a role model for future behaviors. Those ways that were different from the research included doing activities related to the deceased's occupation, mimicking vocal inflections of the deceased, using the person's trademark phrases, moments of recognizing similar habits, and vulnerable stories about the deceased. My interviews also became a way to re-member the dead. They not only helped interviewees continue a bond with my mother, but also helped them continue bonds with other loved ones who had died.

Interviewees spoke of having visions of and dreams about my mother. Aunt Cindy's story about the balloon was shared many times (chapter 3). Aunt Susie discussed seeing a license plate that read ANN 1122 (November 22 is my birthday) when Sister Sledge's "We Are Family" came on the radio. My father and brother both discussed having dreams in which my mother visited them. My father also reminded me of the situation during my college baccalaureate (chapter 1), when sunlight shone through a stained-glass church window and only on me. One of my aunts and a few of my mother's friends discussed how butterflies often appeared whenever my mother was mentioned (chapter 3). My stepmom told me a story about a red rose bush in the backyard that she had been told my mother planted. She said that she had been having a difficult time getting the roses to bloom, but about a week before I returned for my fieldwork, the roses bloomed. She interpreted this as my mother sending a message from Heaven.

As far as observations of possible post-death contact occurring during my fieldwork, there were two mysterious situations that dealt with ants. When I was young, we had an ant problem in our family home. My mother would get frustrated when killing the ants and say, "I hate you fucking ants!" When people would ask me what kind of ants we had in our home, I would respond, "Fucking ants!" In two of my interviews, there was a reference to ants as a sign of post-death contact from my mother. First, on the day of her interview, my aunt told me that she and her husband had gone to the cemetery earlier in the day. They noticed some dirt on my mother's grave, and when they went to clean it off, they saw ants covering the face of the tomb. When I was conducting an interview with two former friends, one of them informed me that they had never had an ant problem in their home, but an hour before I arrived, they had seen several ants around their kitchen sink.

Interviewees also kept many items in their homes to re-member my mother. One woman who had been a client of my mother's would hang a Christmas ornament that held a picture of my mother every year on her tree, and another kept a picture of my mother in her purse. Two other clients, a mother and a daughter, still kept combs my mother gave them, even though the combs were too old to use. A friend of my mother's still tracked all dates associated with my mother on her calendar (her birthday, my mother and father's anniversary, the date of my mother's death). Some family members kept photographs and artifacts that represented my mother in their homes. One of my aunts had framed a picture of a page from an appointment book in which my mother kept records of her clients. Another aunt framed a copy of my mother's obituary and had an angel figurine representing the month of April (the month my mother was born in).

Finally, interviewees addressed practices such as participating in activities my mother would have enjoyed and recognizing her as a role model for future behaviors. One of my uncles started a scholarship fund in my mother's name for a high school graduating senior going into cosmetology. My mother's best friends from her graduating class said they still tried to take trips together as much as possible. My brother, Kyle, stated that he often reflected on my mother's personality and that he strived to be like her in his profession as a diesel fuel and farm equipment salesperson. Kyle also reported that he recognized his difficulty saying no to various requests at work. He knew our mother struggled with this as well, and this encouraged him to seek professional help from a counselor in coping with stress at work.

Although many of the ways to re-member my mother were consistent with those already identified in the research, there were also ways that have not been previously identified. These ways of re-membering were not always explicitly expressed as such. However, they could be classified as re-membering practices. First, many interviewees expressed they often re-membered my mother when doing something with their hair or another person's hair. This suggests that one way to continue a bond with the deceased is to engage in activities related to the person's profession. For example, Pammy, a close family friend, said she would often think of and tell stories about my mother when combing her daughter Addison's hair (even though Addison had never met my mother). A family friend, Jim, even though he was bald, stated his ways of re-membering Mom through his hair:

> She was the only one who knew what to do with me and this bald head. I get up in the morning and look in the mirror and think, *Damn, Ann, we miss you so much*. We loved her so much besides the hair stuff, but you know you just can't help thinking about her that way.

Many of my mother's clients stated they thought of her whenever going to get their hair cut or styled. Although being in a new salon after her death had been painful at first, several of them said, they became more comfortable in this space over time.

Many interviewees discussed how they would use words or phrases that were part of my mother's personal language. One interviewee, Ronna, discussed how her daughter (who is currently a hairdresser) would get confused when giving directions on how to do her hair because of my mom's "language":

> Annie had her own vocabulary when it came to doing hair. She would take "hunky chunkies" out here or there, or she just made her own words, but we all knew what she meant, and we trusted her, and we always loved our hair . . . She also talked about "whispies!" "You don't have whispies out to the side like Farrah Fawcett." "I need to cut your whispies off."

Again, Ronna did not explicitly state that this was a way she re-membered my mother, but by using these ways of speaking, she actively reconstructed my mother's presence into a haircutting moment. One of my aunts stated she always repeated a phrase of my mother's—"Oh, it's just hair!"—whenever a new hairdresser did a botched job. Several interviewees also stated that they remembered a way my mother used to poke fun at herself: whenever she felt that she did not look attractive, my mom would smirk and say, "Pretty!" Interviewees, mostly my mother's sisters, said that they would often do this too.

My mother always kept a disorganized and messy purse. A couple of interviewees, while not strategically keeping a messy purse, said that when others would comment on their purses, they would reference my mother. As one aunt stated:

> I'm standing in the store paying for a Christmas present, and the guy wanted to see the last four digits on my debit card, and I already threw it back in my purse. I didn't put it in the same spot, and I couldn't find it. [My husband] John goes, 'Jesus Christ. Your sister will never be gone.' I started laughing, and I had to dump my purse on the counter. But I never find my car keys in the same place. I can't find nothing in it, and John starts calling me Edith, like he did your mom.

Edith, a character in the 70s sitcom *All in the Family*, is the sweet but scatterbrained wife of the main character, Archie Bunker. My uncle and a few other interviewees stated they would call my mother Edith too. Whenever their wives did something similar to my mother, they would call them Edith. This could be seen as a way to honor my mother's sweet but sometimes scattered personality.

Also, the phrase "cow titties" was used among interviewees. My mother was a fairly buxom woman and would refer humorously to her "cow titties." Some interviewees expressed that they still used this phrase when referring to either their own breasts or the breasts of other women. My mother had a particular term for when she had to take a really intense poop. She called these experiences "blasters," and interviewees humorously reported that they also used this term.

Furthermore, the ways in which my mother pronounced and emphasized words were implicitly used as ways to re-member her. My mother had a specific way of pronouncing my father's name (Lindon) and grandmother's name (Jo-Ann). She would pronounce Lindon "Lynn-duhn" and Jo-Ann "JO-ayun." Several interviewees would recount these vocal inflections in interviews, and while none stated they did this to re-member Mom, at times throughout the interview I heard them mimic these inflections. Interviewees also commented on the way my mother pronounced the words "wash" as "warsh," "milk" as "melk," and "idea" as "ideal."

The recognition of words, phrases, pronunciations, and vocal inflections came from many entertaining stories about my mother. Telling stories about the deceased has been identified as a way to continue a bond with them. However, people usually share stories that valorize the deceased. My interviewees did share stories that emphasized the goodness of my mother's character, but they also told stories about her that might not have portrayed her in the best way. I got many interesting, and sometimes unexpected, responses to questions such as "Tell me a story about Ann as a mother, daughter, hairdresser, patient, etc."

To begin with, my mother's overuse of the word "fuck" was commented on, although not in a disapproving way. One interviewee stated, "It was always 'F this!' And 'F that!' I don't know how you kids didn't always say it." Other stories commented on some of my mother's humorous blunders as a hairdresser. One interviewee discussed how a particular brand of hair color broke out her scalp, and my mother frantically checked on her the following day. One of her sisters told two humorous stories about how my mother dealt with local law enforcement. In the first story, my mother was pulled over for not posting an updated license sticker by police officer Donny Bear, who was the husband of one of her good friends. She retrieved the sticker from her glove compartment and said, "Fuck you, Bear. I got the sticker right here!" In the second story, my mother got out of a speeding ticket by lying to a police officer about feeling as though she was going to throw up. When recounting the event to others, she had jokingly stated, "I'm not hot enough to flirt, so I had to play sick." Other humorous stories included my mother's shampoo basin falling off the wall when she was shampooing a customer's hair, my mother being stressed about customers seeing her messy house, her wild driving, and an instance when she peed on the side of the road during a high school road trip.

However, there were several instances in which stories were not humorous and focused on my mother during her illness. I sensed a few family members had a compulsive need to talk about my mother's illness. For example, on the way home from lunch, one of my aunts spent thirty minutes recounting her experiences of caring for my mother. She kept speaking without leaving any room for me to respond. When she had finished her story, she stated, "It was difficult for me to discuss these things for a while, but now I can, and you are old enough to hear about them."

After completing this research, I felt as though I knew that my mother lived a good life. Many interviewees had shared stories that demonstrated her dedication to her family, clients, and community.

However, the question as to whether she had a "good death" (Schenck & Roscoe, 2009) continued to haunt me. The story of my mother's illness and death did not have as much coherence as the story of her life—they were what Frank (1995) describes as a "chaos narrative." The plot of the chaos narrative is one in which the ill person imagines life will never get better. Although pituitary tumors are fairly common, the way in which my mother's turned cancerous and metastasized to other parts of the body is not common.

The way my family members narrated her illness was consistent with a Western biomedical model of progress. Instead of considering my mother's illness terminal and seeking forms of palliative care, they saw it as something that could be cured or "beaten." We desperately sought a restitution narrative, one that focuses on how the ill individual will recover and go back to his or her "normal" life through means of medical technologies (Frank, 1995). My family's unflinching certainty that we could craft a restitution narrative for my mother made her death even more shocking. During my research, many interviewees wanted to discuss and tell stories about her moments of illness. Perhaps they were trying to salvage my mother's final chapter of life. Perhaps they were attempting to transform a chaos narrative into a quest narrative, one in which the individual and family accepts illness and learns a lesson from the experience. Perhaps these are things I even attempted to do through this work because I felt that my mother did not die a good death.

My mother's illness was never spoken of as terminal. One reason for this might have been a lack of information about the condition of her illness. Another might have been my family's strong denial of death ever being a possibility. Regardless, the opportunity to engage in creative narrative work in shaping a good final chapter of life for my mother was missed.

Although I cannot continue to dwell on what we could have done, it is my hope that this book will facilitate for others a good death through re-membering practices. Hedtke & Winslade (2004) do describe how re-membering not only helps individuals grieve but also helps the dying and their loved ones. They argue that re-membering conversations with the dying can go beyond funeral arrangements, ethical wills, and life reviews to also "be about asking persons who are dying to select out highlights of life that are worth preserving in memory and ritual observance" (p. 67). Although these conversations can be highly effective, there are many obstacles people may face when attempting them. Family members may fear they will upset the dying person with these conversations, or they may superstitiously fear that speaking about death so openly will hasten it. Hedtke and Winslade also argue that caregivers for a dying family member may be so focused on the aspect of loss they may neglect to focus on what need not be lost. If these challenges can be overcome, re-membering conversations may offer peace to the dying person.

THE CHALLENGES AND FAILURES OF CONTINUING BONDS

Grief after death can be a difficult emotion—not only because facing life without someone you love is painful, but also because we live in a death-denying culture (Becker, 1973; Kellehear, 1984; Seale, 1998; Tucker, 2009; Zimmerman & Rodin, 2004). During family gatherings, conversations about death have been referred to as "the elephant in the room" or "the horse on the dining-room table" (Kalish, 1981, cited in Corr & Corr, 2013). Often family members are aware of death's presence, but they are uncomfortable and not sure how to discuss it. As Becker (1973) once argued, "The idea of death, the fear of it, haunts the human animal like nothing else; it is a mainspring of human activity designed largely to avoid the fatality of death, to overcome it by denying in some way that it is the final destiny of man" (p. ix). Because of this silence, many terminally ill individuals' concerns are silenced, and their families are less prepared when death happens.

Part of this cultural death denial could be attributed to increased life expectancies in countries such as the United States. Major advances in life-sustaining treatment for individuals with terminal illness, often resulting in length of life being privileged over quality of life, could be another reason for the denial. Some physicians are socialized to treat death as failure (Hegedus, Zana, & Szabo, 2008)—something to resist and avoid. Many people may choose neither to face death nor to talk about the topic with others and feel apathetic toward their own imminent mortality. Furthermore, death-denying culture can influence the way people cope with the death of a loved one. Talking about the deceased may serve as a reminder that modern medicine cannot overcome every patient's tragic circumstance. If bereaved individuals continue to incorporate the deceased's presence into their lives, they may be told they are depressed or not over the loss. Although these attributions may be made out of care or concern for the bereaved, they also might be made because of societal fear and the taboo topic of death itself.

Sometimes, I struggled with how people responded to my research. I appreciated the comments that were affirmative and when people told me that my doing this research was a great tribute to my mother. The comments that made me uncomfortable came from interviewees who said that this research "must be so therapeutic for me" and that it was a great way for me to cope with my grief. These comments undermined the project. Also, some interviewees had difficulty remembering things about Mom's life. This may have been because of the passage of a decade since my mother's death, or it may have been because these interviewees had more relational distance from her than others. In a few interviews, sometimes an interviewee's response would lack detail. Or, when I asked interviewees whether there were specific ways they memorialized my mother, I got blank stares or I sensed that they struggled to find something meaningful to say.

However, every person I sought for an interview accepted the invite with enthusiasm, except one woman named Kate. She had been a neighbor and close friend of my mother's. After a week of not receiving a response, I assumed Kate was not interested in participating in the study. I was not offended, because I thought she might find participation too difficult. But then Kate came unexpectedly to our family home. "I can't help you with this death and dying stuff," she said.

Although surprised, I was still able to respond to Kate. I told her that if an interview would be too painful, she did not have to participate. I also stated that I had enough people helping me with the project. Still, she talked for twenty-five minutes about how she loved my mother and how my mother was a great person. She concluded by stating, "I feel like we could have done more." I said that I appreciated her help taking care of Mom and that I felt as though everyone had done everything they could. I made sure to visit Kate before I left the field, to make sure this project had not harmed her. Although she did not discuss my mother or the project, she seemed happy to see me.

Some individuals seemed ideal to interview, but I chose not to interview them because of their personal grieving process. My grandmother, my mother's mother, was one example. Although I did engage in several informal conversations with her, I noticed the intensity of her emotionality when even mentioning my mother's name. During my fieldwork, my grandmother was admitted to an assisted living facility due to issues with her memory. Instead of interviewing my grandmother, I decided to use my knowledge about continuing bonds to help her cope with her grief. For example, she told me she did not wish to attend Sunday morning worship services at the facility. She still heard some of the music from the services in her room, including the hymn "How Great Thou Art." This song upset her because it had been played during my mother's funeral procession.

In attempting to help her reframe the music, I asked, "Do you ever think maybe it's a way that Mom tries to let you know she's around?" She seemed to halfheartedly accept this interpretation. In subsequent phone conversations, she does not talk about my mother. If she does, it is not to re-member her but to talk about her grief. It is still difficult for her to ever mention my mother's name.

It seems that the death of a child could be a challenging situation for continuing a bond with the deceased. As many bereavement researchers argue, the death of a child is very difficult because it defies a perceived natural order of life (Becvar, 2001; Gamino, Sewell, & Easterling, 1998; Klass, 1997). I believe that my grandmother will eventually find comfort in re-membering and continuing bonds with the deceased. She confided to me one evening that she still kept my mother's cell-phone number in her phone's contacts list. "I just can't bear to erase it," she said. In her mourning process, I do not feel it is my place to prescribe behaviors that have worked for me. While not outwardly expressing continued bonds with others, my grandmother may still continue bonds in her own way. Allowing herself to cry and feel her grief may be a way she continues a bond with my mother, and she may prefer to do this privately. At the very least, this project helped me see that she may not re-member in the ways I do. It also heightened my awareness of my grandmother's potential emotional states and ways in which I can improve and appreciate our relationship.

It may not always be helpful for some people to continue a relationship with the deceased and maintain their membership status. Hedtke & Winslade (2004) write:

> There may be times when it does not serve a person to remember in ways that reinstate the deceased person, or restore privileged membered status. To do so could create further harm for the person who is alive. In these

circumstances, it may be of benefit to keep the deceased person's membership further away and to build remembering around a more distant, less intimate membership position.

(p. 112)

The utility of keeping the dead at a distance became apparent in my explorations of re-membering processes and their connections to my relationship with my stepmother, Kelly. In interviews with my mother's friends, a few stated they thought Kelly seemed uncomfortable whenever they mentioned my mother. I decided to explore their concerns by interviewing my stepmother.

My stepmother had not been a close friend of my mother's, but she had been a client for a brief time. When my father started dating her, she told me that he worried a lot about people in our community thinking he was dating too soon. She and other interviewees mentioned that my father talked about my mother quite a bit the first few months they were dating. A couple with whom they were friends even expressed that the talk was excessive—to the point where they were uncomfortable on double dates. My father said that he would mention specific dates related to my mother (e.g., her birthday, their wedding anniversary) the first few years that he and Kelly were together. Over the years, he stated that he still sometimes thought about these days but that he did not mention them. When I asked why he felt the need to not mention them, he said that he had moved on. He also stated that he would find Kelly mentioning dates associated with her ex-husband inappropriate, even though he was still alive.

In my interview with Kelly, I surprisingly found that what bothered her wasn't so much the amount of time spent talking about and remembering Mom as how certain family members treated her as a result of my mother's death. I tried to ease into asking her questions about how she managed the tension of my mother's absence in our family. I stated, "I try to put myself in your position. For instance, if I were to marry someone who had lost his first spouse, how would I handle that? What would be required of me?" Kelly responded by saying that she knew what she was getting into when she started dating and eventually married my father. "There are certain things I have to deal with. That's the way it is." When they started dating, she said, my father expressed a lot of guilt that it had been my mother who died. Kelly stated that he told her he thought my mother would have been a better parent. This troubled Kelly and did create some conflict in their relationship.

However, I was shocked to hear about how some family members had treated Kelly since my mother's death. One family member would always send a text to my father on my mother's birthday but would never wish Kelly a happy birthday. Another instance in which Kelly said she felt uncomfortable was during a family trip to visit me in Tampa. She was on the beach when one of my aunts started crying and said that she missed her best friend. When Kelly asked who this best friend was, my aunt stated that it was my mother. And at a family wedding, the mother of the bride asked Kelly if she would take a family picture that included my father, my brother, and me. To Kelly, this act implied her exclusion from the family. I realized that should a person choose to conceptualize a relationship with a deceased parent or spouse and intensely continue that bond, there may be challenges to a relationship with a stepparent. The challenges may be similar to those experienced in situations of divorce where the ex-husband or ex-wife is still living. Some of these challenges may have less to do with the deceased individual than they do with how family members treat the new spouse.

Trying to continue a relationship with the deceased does not always work. First, the contextual factors of the death may make it too emotionally challenging, as it was for Kate and also my grandmother. Societal prescriptions and "feeling rules" for grief, accompanied by a death-denying culture, may make it taboo to speak of the deceased many years after death. The absence of continuing a relationship with the deceased so many years after the death may also affect re-membering practices, should surviving family members attempt to perform them. Having not kept the deceased's presence active, it may be more difficult later on to construct a relationship, especially if details about the deceased have been forgotten.

Family members who want to continue a relationship may have difficulties doing so if they were young when the loved one died. After my mother died, I found that although my younger brother did wish to re-member her, he did not have as many memories as I did, and so I often helped him maintain this relationship. Fear of making other family members uncomfortable may also prevent a continued relationship with the deceased, as it did for my stepmother. It may be best to conceptualize continuing bonds as a narrative blueprint for living rather than a coping strategy. If grieving is conceptualized as an indefinite process, investing too much in continuous bonds as a "quick fix" may not be helpful, especially during times of intense sadness. Even years after my mother's death, there was ample proof that expressions of emotion could still be very intense.

Emotions During Interviews and Challenges to Cultural "Feeling Rules"

When deconstructing the social construction of closure, Berns argues:

> Closure is in particular a fraud on the bereaved, as it preaches that there will—there should—come a moment when grief is over. In reality, though we may go on with our lives, remarry, bear new children, and laugh at silly jokes again, there is no reason ever to stop mourning or to forget what we have lost. Grief may recede; instead of being the ocean we swim in, it may be the vial of ocean water in the cabinet of wonder, but it is always there. Balance yes; closure, never.
>
> (2011, p. 51)

Berns's arguments apply to how the people I interviewed seemed to cope with my mother's death. Even after ten years, interviewees showed open and intense expressions of grief. Also, I was aware of how my own emotionality would fluctuate during the research process. Rarely during interviews would I express emotion, but either while transcribing or reflecting on them, I would cry. Even though I feel no shame in expressing my emotions, professional socialization norms about the researcher role could have conditioned me to stifle the emotions I felt.

Some of my interviewees recounted moments when they, or others, violated cultural "feeling rules" for grief. One of my aunts, an elementary school teacher, discussed being approached by the school janitor (an acquaintance of my mother's) at a parent-teacher conference:

> The janitor said, "Oh. How's Kyle and Blake? What are they doing now?" and then she said, "Oh, I miss Ann so much," and she starts crying, and I'm thinking, . . . *I don't remember her babysitting you kids.* But she starts *crying crying crying*, and I said I think about her all the time.

Another interviewee, a former client, discussed her expressions of emotion during her first hair appointment after my mother died:

> It was bad. Really bad. I was crying in the waiting room. I still go to the same place. I'm loyal when I find someone I like. But I remember crying on the way there, crying in the waiting room, and the whole time she's cutting my hair. I hate to be one of those people who constantly apologizes. But I kept saying, "I'm sorry. I'm sorry." I must have apologized at least thirty times. And then I felt the need to explain why I'm crying, so I said that my hairdresser just died and I was close to her, like family but not family. It wasn't the first time, though—that was the worst. I fought crying the next two or three haircuts. The thing that was odd is I didn't know that I was going to cry.

This interviewee had been surprised that she reacted in this way to her first appointment, perhaps alluding to the idea that she thought she had "moved on" from my mother's death. I could empathize with this need to move on, as I had similar feelings for eight years after my mother's death.

Furthermore, interviewing friends and family about the death and re-membering of my mother created a rather complex position for me as a researcher. There were many times I could easily empathize with them, but there were times I was surprised about things they said during an interview. I learned that often I needed to focus less on what to say and more on just listening. Some interviewees had been withholding emotions (aside from grief) for some time, and it appeared that my presence and research project provided a means for them to express these emotions.

One emotion that surprised me was guilt. In the first of two examples, one interviewee recalled how she was feeling with her family on Christmas Eve, just five days after my mother's passing:

> I can remember coming into the living room . . . I remember my Christmas tree was up, and all three kids were there. I remember feeling guilty and thinking, *She's not going to get to have this!* I hate that when someone dies you make it about you. I felt selfish for making it about me. You'd think I was Catholic the way I feel guilt about everything!

I reassured her that it was normal to feel grateful that she would be able to share these experiences with her children.

Another interviewee, who had a health condition similar to my mother's, stated:

> There's been a lot of guilt in me about why God took your mother and left me. Because I feel like she had a lot more to give than what I did. She loved life so much, and I don't understand. To my knowledge, the pituitary tumors are rare, and then you have two people who are the same age that have the same tumor. Why did hers make this happen and mine did not? I've still maintained mine. I still have to go to the doctor. I still have to take medicine every two weeks. Why couldn't they do that for Annie?

Although it is not uncommon for the bereaved to experience guilt, it is unique that these two interviewees had been clients of my mother's. Just as there may not be an expected timetable for the grieving process, there may not be a clear demarcation between who feels and who doesn't feel guilt.

However, I did have difficulty responding to some reactions. One interviewee, who had been a client of my mother's and had helped care for her, said she was angry. When I asked toward whom and about what, I was surprised to find that she was angry with my mother. I asked her why she felt like this, and she responded by saying, "I was just angry." Not sure what to say, I changed the topic. My father also expressed anger when he stated that he was "fucking angry" at my mother for leaving him. In both examples, I interpret their emotions as not so much anger at my mother as anger at the situation. If one believes that a relationship with the deceased can exist, his or her misguided anger could be projected onto the deceased just as if they were still living.

My interviewees' behaviors suggest that traditional "feeling rules" for grief in the United States were not always followed, and there were breaches in the cultural scripts. The interview process became a way to re-member my mother, and, through these processes, cultural "feeling rules" for grief and the divide between the living and the dead were queered (Paxton, 2014). My interviewees' responses showed that a dichotomy of either moving on from a loss or staying stuck in the emotional trauma is a limited way to view the grieving process. During some interviews, I was immersed in my interviewees' grief over my mother's death, but in many of those moments, there was relational growth and insight into my mother's experiences with illness. For example, I learned from my mother's clients and friends that my mother was more aware of her possible death than I had originally conceptualized. She also may have been supportive of my sexuality.

Through re-membering my mother during interviews, interviewees assisted me in re-membering myself back into my hometown. We also helped each other re-member ourselves back into some past relationships that had gone stagnant. Several interviewees actively maintained a bond with my mother, and some did not. For those who did choose to have this relationship (either through their own strategies or through assisting me during the research process), it did not completely "resolve" grief that they had felt in the past or currently felt. Rather, the research process encouraged some interviewees to feel more comfortable in their grief and about the bonds they sustained with people, both the living and the dead.

CHAPTER 5

FUTURE DIRECTIONS FOR CONTINUING BONDS RESEARCH

Root & Exline (2014) urge researchers to include the following concerns in their future studies on continuing bonds with the deceased: providing a more specific definition for what counts as a continuing bond; the bereaved's perception of the bond as positive or negative; the quality of the pre-death relationship; and the bereaved's beliefs about the afterlife. More specifically, they argue, "An important next step in continuing bonds research is to assess the bereaved individual's subjective experience associated with the continued bond expression, as well as the bereaved's interpretation of the meaning of the expression—in particular what the expression signifies about the bereaved, about the deceased, and about their relationship" (p. 5). Thus far, I have attempted to show this through my autoethnographic work.

While immersed in the analysis of my interviews, I determined several directions for continuing bonds research that could help enrich our understanding of subjective experiences of grief. These directions include the role of social media in continuing bonds, continuing bonds implications for voluntary kin, and how continuing bonds with the dead can improve relationships with the living. In this final chapter, I summarize these future possibilities for research and provide a brief reflection on my overall experiences of continuing bonds through the research process.

THE ROLE OF SOCIAL MEDIA IN CONTINUING BONDS

"There isn't wifi in heaven!" An interviewee made this statement in a study on Facebook memorial pages (Marwick & Ellison, 2012). In recent years, social networking sites (SNSs) have changed the ways in which people interact with one another. Much research has been done on how SNSs affect the many facets of social life, including impression management and friendship performance, network structure, bridging online and offline social networks, and privacy (Boyd & Ellison, 2008). Some researchers have taken an interest in how the Internet is changing the ways we think about loss (Sofka, Noppe Cupit, & Gilbert, 2012). Some of this work has addressed how SNSs serve as a way for people to continue bonds with the deceased. However, more work can be done in the area of what has been coined "thanatechnology."

Sofka et al. (2012) define thanatechnology as "all types of communication technology that can be used in the provision of death education, grief counseling, and thanatology research" (p. 3). In regard to thanatology research, much work has been done on how online communication technology has impacted grief and mourning. Walter, Hourizi, Moncur, & Pitsillides (2011) provide an overview of how the Internet has changed "how we die and mourn" (p. 275). They first argue that the web has changed the dying process through the formation of online support groups and the use of blogs (in which those who are dying can archive their experiences). Sofka et al.'s study suggests that communication technology can change the way we experience funerals—whether by allowing individuals to Skype into services from various locations or by providing online guest books. Furthermore, memorializing practices are changing through communication technology—including the creation of web cemeteries and Facebook memorial pages.

In October 2009, Facebook's head of security, Max Kelly, announced the site's memorialization policy (Fletcher, 2009): If a family member dies, you must fill out a form and provide a link to an obituary. This will allow the profile to become memorialized, so that it no longer turns up in public searches and friend suggestions to other users. Only close family members and friends are then able to post on the wall of the deceased. Some individuals have the deceased's account deleted and instead create a separate page for memorialization. However, Facebook's memorialization policy is not mandatory, and it is possible for anyone to operate a dead person's profile if he or she knows the username and password.

Many studies on the use of Facebook memorializing focus on teens and college students. Through interviewing college students who had lost a close friend, Hieftje (2012) identified several salient themes for

FUTURE DIRECTIONS FOR RESEARCH

Facebook memorialization. College students used Facebook memorial pages to sustain feelings of connection with the deceased by looking through old photo albums, wall posts, and private messages. These students would also post messages directly to the deceased on the memorial pages. Finally, the interviewees used the memorial pages as a way to commemorate the life of the deceased. For example, one student posted a running slide show with pictures of the deceased, set to his favorite music.

Some studies have focused on the frequency of posts after someone has died. Williams & Merten (2009) reviewed 20 profiles of dead adolescents between 2005 and 2007. They found that the number of posts decreased every month after the individual's death—from close to 80 posts one month after the death to 10 or fewer posts after a year. There were more comments on significant dates such as birthdays and anniversaries of the death. Adolescent posters would sometimes provide meta-commentary about the posts, too. The topics covered in online comments included the funeral of the deceased, seeing the deceased's body, and the possibility of an afterlife. Finally, commentary about the cause of death was highly prevalent; for example, in a case of suicide, one comment was "I wish you would have told us you were hurting."

Not all of these online studies have focused solely on adolescents' experiences. Marwick & Ellison (2012) found many of the same occurrences, including direct communication with the deceased through posts, with older populations. Some users would hold competitions to see if they could get a certain number of "likes" on the memorial pages. Furthermore, people would create memorial pages not only to honor the deceased but also to promote a certain cause related to the death (for example, to stop bullying in schools). Those who made specific memorial pages instead of memorializing the deceased's profile had to regulate posts more frequently, such as when a page manager had to intervene when "trolls" left derogatory remarks about the deceased. So, while there was more potential for activity on memorial pages, there had to be more regulation. DeGroot (2012) noted that Facebook members could use memorial pages to directly communicate with the deceased. These messages served two functions: (1) to make sense of the death and (2) to continue a bond.

April 29, 2014, would have been my mother's fiftieth birthday. Out of a desire to reconnect with her and my curiosity about the role of social networking and re-membering the deceased, I created a Facebook event page for her birthday. The page's title was "Re-membering Ann Paxton on Her 50th Birthday." I created the event a week before her birthday, and the description read:

> On Tuesday, April 29, 2014, my mother would have been 50 years old. I am a strong supporter of the belief that it is possible to continue a relationship with the deceased even though they are no longer physically present. I am inviting you to celebrate 50 years of my mother's loving presence over the next week. Feel free to post a fond memory or story on this event wall. If you never met my mother, you can still post whatever you are emotionally moved to post. Confirming attendance to this event just means you are re-membering Mom on her birthday in whatever way you choose. Thanks in advance to those participating.

I invited close to two hundred of my Facebook friends, some of whom had met my mother.

Responses to this event varied, from deeply moving to oddly troubling. Of the total number of guests invited, 104 confirmed attendance, 89 did not respond, and one person said she would maybe attend. This "maybe" response was from a high school acquaintance of mine. Her response and the lack of response from others caused some friction with attendees. For example, one of my cousins posted on the event wall:

> Ok so there were 100 invited and 92 going and 1 MAYBE! Really????!!! Sorry to offend anybody but I think that's crazy in this situation. Did they even read the description?? "Confirming attendance to this event just means you are re-membering Mom on her birthday in whatever way you choose. Thanks in advance to those participating."

For my cousin, the lack of response was offensive. To ease the tension, I responded with the following post:

> I wouldn't take it as an insult. I tend to not look at Facebook events as much as I should. Some people might have seen the title and assumed I was doing something in Tampa. Some people I sent the invite to didn't know Mom. I hope that no matter what level of participation, this highlights the

possibility of continuing a relationship with the deceased. Thank you for
your comment though.

My cousin responded, "Sorry. I just feel passionate about this! She was
the greatest and I miss her soooo much!" Her response not only confirmed a commitment to a continued relationship with my mother, but
also showed her love for me. My uncle added to the comment thread and
wrote, "I agree. Come on Cindy, Patty, and Harry [my mother's siblings]!
Time to join social media. What would it hurt?"

Some of the attendees decided to post something right after joining.
These posts were shorter and more general. Here are some examples:

> "Such a sweet lady! ☺"
> "I remember her infectious laugh! Couldn't help but smile when you heard
> it." "Miss her. She was such a sweet lady!"
> "She and Lisa were a hoot together..."

A friend in my mother's graduating class made this last comment. I do
not know who Lisa is, but I assume she was another friend of my mother's group. Re-membering rituals on social media may give participants
a sense of freedom in their posts, and they may not feel the obligation to
fully explain a message.

One of my friends who had never met my mother posted:

> Great way to remember your mom! My favorite memory is all of the times
> we laughed telling stories of little Blake eating snacks and watching her cut
> hair. I know she would be very proud of the man that little guy has grown
> into! Sending my love your way, and to your mom. XOXO

This post showed me that people can actively participate in re-membering the deceased even if they never met them. It also helped me recognize
how many times in the past I had actively re-membered my mother with
others.

One attendee of the event messaged me the day before my mother's
birthday, and she seemed distraught. She wrote, "Can't be there tomorrow. My husband's mother is being transferred to a care center for short
term, and I need to be with him. I do want to share an 'Ann' story." This

FUTURE DIRECTIONS FOR RESEARCH

person interacted with me as if my mother were still alive. She shared with me the following story about Mom:

> It was a well-known fact (confirmed by your Mom) that she didn't like house cleaning. One day she walked in to work and announced that a person could eat off her kitchen floor. I congratulated her on having clean floors. She said, "No, no . . . my floor has so much food on it you could literally have a meal!" LOL!!! To this day, when I clean my kitchen floor I always think of Ann. Her sense of humor will be with us forever.

I posted this publicly, because I wanted to help fulfill her wish to be a part of the event, but I also felt the story offered a sense of my mother's personality.

The most posting activity occurred on the actual day of my mother's birthday. Some individuals uploaded pictures of my mother or of themselves with my mother to accompany their messages. Many of the stories were about my mother as a family member or a hairdresser. Here is one hairdresser post:

> If you know me you know that I change my hair color all the time (I'm a do-it yourselfer). For Ann it was a funny joke—I remember one night in particular that I decided I wanted red hair. I colored it and when I was done I looked like the girl from the musical Annie—my hair was orange! I had to call Ann and she had to "see" what I had done! When I got to Ann's she took one look at it and started singing "The Sun Will Come Up Tomorrow" and then laughed that incredible laugh! After she finished laughing, she gave me color to fix my screw up! When Joe would go to Ann's shop and girls would ask what he thought of their hair color Ann would say, "You're taking an opinion from a man whose wife changes her hair color like she changes underwear!" So here's to Ann—Happy 50th Birthday! We love and miss you every day!

Another post:

> Blake, what a wonderful way to celebrate your mother. I too was a client of the Cater Vend beauty shop. She would wrap my head in toilet paper when she would run out of the beauty supply batting while giving me a perm. She would joke I only do this for my most favorite customers! Once she

136

FUTURE DIRECTIONS FOR RESEARCH

even dropped the lid to the shampoo bowl while my head was still in it! We about peed our pants laughing so hard! Ann was fun! She had a wonderful way of drawing people in and leaving them with a smile.

Some posts discussed Ann both as a hairdresser and as a family member:

One of my funniest memories with Ann was every single time she did my hair (braiding, styling) if she would pull my hair and I would go "ouchhh" she would instantly respond "oh wahhh wahhh go cry to your other favorite aunts" haha it would shut me up every time. She would look at me and give me one of her warm smiles after she said it. If only she really knew how much she meant to me. She was the funniest and most loving aunt a person could have. She is missed every day in the Johnson household.

Another post:

So many memories with that sweet lady!! I used to love going to Cater-Vend for a haircut, but the start of a new school year was my absolute favorite. That was when I got my "back-to-school PERM." Aunt Annie would always do that one on the house! I used to rock some big-ass hair with huge bangs teased & sprayed. Now I have a daughter of my own, with a head full of natural curls. We rock big-ass hair everyday :)

These posts suggest that when engaging in re-membering processes, public and private sphere blur, and people may even celebrate a deceased individual's humorous blunders on the job. This information may be useful for organizational communication research in showing how if one is highly skilled in interpersonal communication, customers may overlook mistakes. In my mother's case, some customers not only overlooked these mistakes but found humor in them and a way to cope with her death.

Throughout the day, attendees posted comments and pictures on the event wall and engaged in conversation about these posts. I announced different activities I was doing for Mom's birthday, including checking in at a restaurant for "Ann's Birthday Dinner" and posting a picture of myself drinking her favorite beverage, an Amaretto and Sprite, at a local bar. There were five posts made a day after the birthday, and one was made almost a month later.

137

Since the creation of this event, no other online memorials have been created for Mom—although Facebook friends continue to send private messages about re-membering her. This specific birthday event was often brought up in my interviews, and, when it was discussed, interviewees highly praised it. It also inspired some to talk about other ways that social media had been used to continue relationships with deceased family members and friends. In one interview, there was some criticism about how certain family members were using Facebook to memorialize the deceased. One interviewee expressed her discomfort over family members keeping her brother's Facebook page active and acting as him. The family member would make status updates in the first person, and the interviewee thought that was "creepy." Another interviewee discussed how a friend used a memorial page to mourn the loss of his partner but that the posts went "on and on for months."

There are various reactions to continuing bonds and re-membering through social media, dependent upon length of time after death, audience, and online context of the re-membering strategy (keeping the dead's profile active versus creating a memorial page). As social media continue to blur the lines between the public and private worlds, it might blur the lines between the living and the dead. Although it was apparent that an online context had an effect on the ways people formed bonds with the deceased, I found that sustaining healthy bonds with the deceased improved the quality of my relationships with the living.

Re-Membering, Voluntary Kin, and Biological Ties: Strengthening Bonds of the Living Through the Dead

Braithwaite et al. (2010) discuss communication scholarship that explores formations of families outside of a nuclear and biological framework. In the past, these types of families have been described variously but most often as "fictive kin" (Chatters, Taylor, & Jayakody, 1994; Ibsen & Klobus, 1972; Muraco, 2006, as cited in Braithwaite et al., 2010). Braithwaite et al. write, "Fictive families are most often referred to by scholars as what they are not; that is, they are defined by how they are different from the conventional understanding of family, focusing on what fictive family members lack" (p. 390). Braithwaite et al. challenge this label and choose to use "voluntary kin," implying a "mutuality of selection." They developed several typologies on how voluntary

FUTURE DIRECTIONS FOR RESEARCH

kin families occur and the emotional benefits interviewees receive from them. One of these typologies designated voluntary kin as substitute family. These families form when members established a relationship due to death of or estrangement from biological family members. An example of voluntary kin as substitute family was that, after one interviewee lost her only son in a car accident, one of the son's close friends became like a son to her.

It may be pertinent to explore how forms of voluntary kin help continue a bond with a deceased family member. I have a very close relationship with my doctoral advisor, Dr. Carolyn Ellis. Types of advisor-advisee relationships vary, but ours feels very much like that of a mother and son. We chat about my work but also aspects of our personal lives, she has invited me over to her home for dinner, and I refer to her as my academic mother. This type of relationship, a form of voluntary kin, not only provides emotional support but also helps me continue a relationship and re-member my biological mother. I know that I can talk openly and often about my mother with Carolyn. I can also share with her stories of possible post-death contact—stories I worry other people might criticize me for telling.

One example of being able to share a story happened during the final stages of the writing process for my dissertation. One evening I was plagued by the typical worries of a graduate student—finishing my dissertation, trying to publish another article, and being on the academic job market—and had trouble sleeping. After tossing and turning for a few hours, I decided to start my day early and work on the dissertation. While getting my coffee ready, I spotted a bottle of maple syrup that I had not used in a long time. I wondered when the syrup was going to expire and checked the expiration date: April 29, 2015. This is my mother's birthday. Then, when I logged onto my computer, I received a notification on Facebook that it was Carolyn's birthday.

What made this coincidence even more peculiar was an online exchange I had had with Carolyn a few days before. My mother's friends from her graduating class decided to take a trip to celebrate their fiftieth birthdays. This was the same group of friends I interviewed (chapter 4) who took a cruise for their fortieth birthdays. I had sent a Facebook message to a couple of these women telling them that my mother would have appreciated them still going on trips together. I sent Carolyn a message as well about this, and I thanked her for helping me find what mattered to me in terms of academic scholarship. She responded by saying many affirmative things, including that she thought it was an honor that I called her my academic mother. Carolyn said that she felt that she and my mother would have gotten along wonderfully and taken great joy in co-parenting me.

And so, I was excited to tell Carolyn about these strange coincidences. This was not the first time I shared with her stories of my beliefs in contact from the deceased. Carolyn enjoys these stories and listens carefully. I think, regardless of our differing spiritual beliefs, they help us feel closer to each other. They also help me feel closer to my mother.

It's important to consider how continuing bonds can influence relationships with biological family, friends, and fellow community members as well. One of the strongest improvements I had in a relationship as a result of engaging in the process of continuing bonds was with my father. As depicted in this book, I was close with my mother. Because of our financial circumstances, both parents worked. My father often spent long hours in the coal mine—putting massive strain on his body and getting little sleep. The time I had with him at home was limited, and often (although this was understandable) he was irritable. We had few common interests, and I never felt as though we would be very close.

I had tried to improve my relationship with my father before I discovered the process of continuing bonds. I first found some guidance in Adams's (2006) article about his troubled relationship with his father. In describing this relationship, he writes, "I'm a victim; so is my father. I'm an oppressor; so is he. We victimize and oppress together; simultaneously hurting and being hurt while never deciding to quit. We're both seeking love. Maybe we're both in love. Somehow" (p. 705). This sentiment resonated with me. Until reading that article, I had often attributed many of the problems in my relationship with my father to him. I had always blamed him for our issues. Adams's work pushed me to think about how my actions were contributing to the negative patterns in the relationship. After reading his work, I continued to reframe my relationship with my father and actively tried to construct positive patterns of interaction.

Continuing a relationship with my deceased mother through my research has aided me in the construction of these positive relational patterns. I found out information about my mother's life and her relationship with my father that I might not have sought out if not for writing this book. For example, although I had heard some details about how

FUTURE DIRECTIONS FOR RESEARCH

my mother and father met, I had not heard the story in its entirety. I also learned about hardships my father went through in order to care for my mother—he had to work in a mine three hours away in order to maintain insurance to pay for her medical care. He felt profound guilt for having to be away from her during times of her illness. This guilt carried on after her death, when he confessed that he went to our family priest and told him he felt somehow he was to blame for her death. While interviews for this project were emotionally intense, I think they proved beneficial for both my father and me. Re-membering my mother through interviews provided us a safe context to open up and share our vulnerabilities with each other.

Similarly, I have seen re-membering facilitate a safe and open space for sharing trauma in the classroom. In several of my classes, I give students a continuing bonds assignment. I ask them to bring in a photograph or item that represents someone who has died or they have lost contact with. They then introduce that person to the class. I ask everyone to sit in a circle and share their presentations. The conversations that result after the presentations have been astounding. Students will discuss common experiences of loss, and they will state how it feels good to know they are not alone in their experiences. Others will discuss how the activity might prepare them for future experiences of loss.

CONCLUDING THOUGHTS

I'd like to think that this story will help many heal from whatever trauma they may undergo, but I do have two specific audiences in mind—those who have lost a loved one and those struggling with their families' acceptance of their sexuality. I already have had individuals approach me about my work. Paul, a close friend, had a strong emotional reaction after reading one of my articles that led to this book (Paxton, 2014). In this article, I construct an imagined conversation with my mother about my sexuality. Paul responded:

> There's a part of me I don't understand/love/am confused by and that makes it hard for me to know how other people would receive me. But reading the conversation with your mom made me realize that she loves you for you and not because of any one aspect of you, since you celebrate you, she celebrates you. As I learn to love myself more and be honest with myself I'll

> be able to realize that people will love me. And if they don't, then they don't love, but they love the lie I've told them.

For me, this message suggests that there is more going on during re-membering than just connecting with the deceased.

Whether I am re-membering through writing about my experiences or through interactive interviews, I am also learning more about my experience through hindsight (Freeman, 2010). I am not really seeing the error of my ways in regard to my past relationship with my mother. Rather, I am seeing how I let certain canonical narratives (Bruner, 1987) of grief and rural space separate me from family members and friends back in my hometown. The narrative that one should move on from a loss and push grief aside and the narrative that says queer individuals are not accepted in rural spaces both impede upon my life story. Through re-storying my life, when I am making myself vulnerable to grief and loss in the presence of others experiencing similar feelings, something transformative happens. I let my defenses down, and I consider the possibility that community members are not rejecting me because of my sexuality. I realize that these individuals (from whom I at one time felt so distanced) not only loved and cared about my mother—they love and care about *me*. Through re-membering my mother, I am also re-membering myself back into my community.

Just as I have realized death does not have to foreclose the narrative of my relationship with my mother, I also realize it does not have to foreclose my relationship with family members and friends in my hometown. Will I ever live in DuQuoin again permanently? I doubt it. However, I should not fear going back. I should not fear the pain of loss or rejection that held me back for so many years.

Furthermore, I have begun wondering about how I want to be remembered after I die. Professionally, I would like to be known for producing research that made a difference—helping people heal from trauma and helping people resolve interpersonal conflicts. As Bochner (2009) argues, we should study things we care about in whatever ways our work will most benefit society. Journal articles, book chapters, and conference presentations are important to my career. However, the number of lines on my CV does not matter if I am not a good, ethical person. I do not want to be known as the son, grandson, brother, nephew, or friend that left, became successful, and never cared about those with whom he

FUTURE DIRECTIONS FOR RESEARCH

grew up. I do not want that narrative thread to be part of my story. Even though there may be differences between me and the community members of DuQuoin, I find strength, encouragement, and compassion in their presence. I would not have known this had it not been for hindsight and processes of re-membering.

I would like to close with a response from an interviewee after reading some of my work:

> Blake I just finished reading your paper. Last night I had a dream and I can't say it was as much of a dream as it was a vision of seeing some of my loved ones that have passed away and one of them was your mom . . . which made me remember your paper . . . and as I sit here typing this with tears in my eyes I want to tell you it's wonderful. Reading and hearing others tell stories about your mom took me back to those days . . . especially the ones about the Hair Loft, your grandpa Corky, and your mom not wanting people to see the messy house. Thanks for allowing us to be a part of this. Your mom would have been so proud of you, I know I am. She was and always will be my best friend.

In these processes of re-membering, we can learn about what it means to live with a story (Frank, 1995) and incorporate loss into daily living. Re-membering can allow us to reflect on and learn from our pasts in order to live better futures. Re-membering processes do not bring the dead back to life in a supernatural or spiritual sense, but, through storytelling and reflection, the dead regain membership in our lives—helping us understand others and ourselves better. What could be more divine?

AFTERWORD
A Family Wedding Reception to Re-Member

The wedding reception for my cousin Ryan and his wife Hillary is outdoors. Since this is his second marriage, the family decided to keep the ceremony simple. The wedding was held earlier in the afternoon, with only immediate family members. The reception is taking place in the yard of his two-story ranch house, located in a rural area of DuQuoin. As my brother and I travel to the reception, past cornfields and on long, winding gravel roads, a thick smell of cow manure permeates the air.

The evening weather is a little chilly for June—in the mid- to upper sixties, with a slight breeze. I shiver as I step out of my father's Ford truck—the "trophy truck," as my mother jokingly called it. He bought it when I was in middle school. The license plate still reads "4 Packy"—Packy being my father's nickname among close friends. When he first bought the truck, he washed and waxed it weekly and was adamant about nobody eating or drinking in it. I giggle when I remember Mom taking it through the car wash, vacuuming up French fries, and saying, "He'll never fucking know!" Such a simple memory can bring her back—even if for only a brief moment.

After a few arguments with my brother about what he should wear and making a quick trip to a clothing store for him to buy dress pants that fit, we've finally made it to Ryan's house. Kelly and Dad, having volunteered to cater the reception, are already here. The evening's meal will

145

be served buffet-style and include my father's famous pulled pork loin. My stomach growls in anticipation.

All six of my mother's brothers and sisters are at the reception with their accompanying families. Hillary's entire family is in attendance, and so are several of their close family members and friends. The wedding colors are turquoise, pink, and white. Aunt Cindy is wearing a turquoise skirt with a black cardigan and a multicolored pewter stone necklace. When she spots my brother and me, she gives us a hug and a kiss on the cheek. I detect a hint of her Liz Claiborne perfume. "Don't forget to sign the guest book!" she says.

As the evening progresses, I find myself being reflexive. The more time goes on, the more difficult it is to gather all the family members, and weddings and funerals are about the only events where this happens. But when family members do come together, familiar feelings of love and comfort ignite.

My father's cooking, as usual, is a hit. Guests go through the line more than once, piling their plates high with traditional Midwest cuisine. My cousin Seth pours me a few too many glasses of red wine. The buzz from the alcohol, mixed with the sounds of my aunts' high-pitched "hyena laughs," makes me feel at peace.

It feels good to be home.

After dinner and a few toasts, the DJ starts the music and beckons guests to the dance floor, which is a concrete driveway in front of Ryan's garage. I jump from my seat when I hear the familiar tune of the "Cupid Shuffle." Aunt Jan is next to me at the table. I turn to her and say, "Come on, Jan! Let's dance."

She crosses her arms and responds, "I don't know this dance."

I pull her out of her seat. "I'll teach you!"

When we reach the dance floor, I'm surprised to find that my father and Kelly have left their serving posts and joined the dancers. Dad usually is particular about the music he listens and dances to. He's more of a country and old rock and roll kind of man, and so I'm pleased to see he's giving the shuffle a try. "Your old man's still got it!" he yells when he sees Jan and me approach.

After the first few rounds of steps, Jan does better than me. I get lost in the music and looking around at fellow dancers. Aunt Cindy is beaming brightly and playfully shaking her hips at my father. Kelly laughs at Cindy's actions, and Aunt Patty whispers something in Cindy's ear that

AFTERWORD

makes her laugh harder. I'm happy to see Kelly among the family. Kyle stands to the side of the dance floor with a big toothy grin. He chats with two female classmates. They're laughing at something he has said, and one of them reaches out and playfully punches his shoulder.

In the last ten years, many things have changed. Family members have married and remarried, grandchildren have been born, other relatives have died, and there have even been a few job changes and relocations. While my aunts believe that my mother was the peacekeeper and glue of the family, I still think they're doing the best they can without her. The same feelings of joy I had at past Strong family events before my mother's death are still here. I've laughed just as a hard and smiled just as much.

And we know how to have a damn good time.

After the shuffle ends, I wipe sweat from my brow and take a break from the dance floor. Several display tables surround the floor. One holds the guest book, and another features pictures of the bride, the groom, their children, and some of the new blended family members. I spot one table I have yet to peruse. I remember that this is the reception memory table. It was my cousin Meredith's idea to have this table. On it are framed pictures of deceased friends and family members we all wish could be here today.

I examine each picture, in particular those of my Grandpa Corky and Mom. She's about twenty-two years old and the maid of honor in Aunt Susie's wedding—adorned in a bright blue dress and a white headband. Her smile is full and framed against the background of a full face with rosy red blushed cheeks. It's the happiest I've ever seen her in a picture, and I'd like to think that this would be the expression she'd have right now, watching the reception unfold.

A chill goes up the back of my neck when I spot a framed message behind the pictures. It says, next to an image of a heart, "We know you would be here today if heaven wasn't so far away."

"But I know you're here, Mom," I say to myself. "I miss you."

As I look back at the dance floor and see the fun my family is having tonight, I wonder if perhaps Heaven could be conceptualized outside of the parameters of a metaphysical space. Maybe instead of Heaven existing above us in some invisible realm, Heaven is the ability to embrace life and to love and feel deeply with others. To understand that while the human experience can be filled with many disappointments and devastation, there is life after a loss. I will never know if there is a God or an afterlife. But there are a few things about which I'm certain.

My mother, even though she died young, led a good and full existence. She tried to teach me many things in my youth, but one lesson is that if you touch just one person in this lifetime you've fulfilled your purpose. It's apparent from this project that she touched many lives—her family, friends, clients, community members. She was not some grand public figure but an everyday woman, a proud mother and beautician with a small salon in her home.

Through continuing a relationship with her, I've been able to continue relationships with those in my life I had neglected. Broken bonds are being restored, and I walk in shame less often.

It feels good to hold joy and sorrow together.

It feels good to know that many people love and accept me.

It is good to feel at home with grief.

APPENDIX
Methodology and Analysis as Mourning

Spinning Selves Autoethnographically

Our relationships, both with the living and with the dead, could be considered cultural artifacts. We can learn much about the norms and values of a given community by looking at how these types of relationships work. In this book, I had many "webs" (Geertz, 1973) of culture to sort through in order to better understand my mother's community of grievers' relationship with her: the culture of my family, the culture of a town, and the culture of bereavement in America. These, along with my academic training, offered complex relational interplays between researcher and interviewees. Although I originally did not consider this project an intervention, I do believe that through the research process, my interviewees and I were able to spin a culture of bereavement together—one that would help us cope with future instances of trauma and loss.

Furthermore, I wanted to provide an autoethnographic account to show these processes of spinning up close and personal. On spinning stories autoethnographically, Berry (2013) writes:

> The processes are too complex, the stakes are too high, to examine from a distance. I offer my story as a voice for others immersed in their own negotiations, and perhaps in need of a story to cling. I convey this story, my spin on spinning, knowing that across our lives, some spins are encouraged and others discouraged, and some spinners are deemed more worthy

of inclusion and love than others. I spin knowing that we are always already spinning, and sometimes in distressing ways.

(p. 211)

Before the research process, I was spinning my bereavement process and community involvement in unproductive ways. The town of DuQuoin represented a space of pain, from my mother's death and a fear of rejection because of my sexuality. These unproductive spinning processes were so frequent and consistent that they seemed to create a web of negativity. This web made me ponder several questions: How was I to ever feel comfortable in my hometown again? How could I mindfully engage in the research process and make sure I respected each interviewee's mourning process and privacy? Would I find myself being stuck again in the trauma of my mother's death? Before entering the field, I was haunted by the thought of offending my mother's community of grievers. I also worried about my own well-being.

I did not have my university's Institutional Review Board (IRB) to cling to for reassurance that I was doing the right things. After submitting my application for review, I received the following response:

> Dear Mr. Paxton, The IRB has determined that the activities described in the application are not designed to be a systemic investigation that will contribute to generalizable knowledge under the criteria required by Health and Human Services. The activities therefore do not constitute research per USF IRB criteria. As a result, IRB approval is not required for this activity. The study is marked closed—never approved. Please see the attached letter from the IRB Chairperson.

I was astonished. I was interviewing human subjects about my mother's death. I was asking them questions that would possibly evoke strong grief and sadness. Even though my goals did not relate to the generalizability of knowledge, why did this exclude my project as legitimate research?

Even without the IRB's assistance, I knew that several lingering questions might finally be answered. These questions were on issues such as whether some of my family and friends would accept me as a gay man, whether my mother thought she was going to die and planned for the end of her life, whether there was anything left unsaid among her and her community of grievers, and whether people had learned to live with the grief from her death in the best way possible. While this research endeavor excited me, I feared it. What if I heard information I did not want to hear? What if I harmed a relationship instead of strengthened it? If I made a mistake, would I be able to return to my hometown again? I knew this project would be messy. However, I was determined to emerge from the field and create webs of culture that would empower and inspire others. Or, at the very least, unweave and loosen the tight web of negativity I had previously spun about my hometown.

THE INVOLVED AND VULNERABLE OBSERVER

In several situations, I considered myself an "involved observer," in which the researcher is required "to be a part of what is being observed, to join in the lives of the people while at the same time seek to understand them and the forces which mold them and to which they respond" (Clark, 1989, as cited in Boylorn, 2012 p. 117). It was not difficult to take part in the events of my interviewees' lives and enter the field, because I had grown up in the community. However, attempting to analyze my hometown's culture was a different endeavor. There were many times I felt a divided sense of self (Bochner, 1997)—the academic and relationally neutral theorist part of me was sometimes at odds with the family member and friend part of me. My interviewees probably saw me in many different ways as well: Blake the researcher, Blake the student, Blake the gay man, and Blake the son of my parents. Some identity labels I embraced comfortably, yet others I was hesitant to disclose. This made me feel like both an involved and a vulnerable observer (Behar, 1996).

Often, during interviews I sensed that I was engaging in processes of covering certain aspects of my identity. To cover, Yoshino (2007) says, is to "tone down a disfavored identity" (p. ix). As depicted earlier in the book, I was surprised by how direct some people were when asking questions about my sexuality. The interviews made me realize that there were certain aspects of my identity that I didn't need to cover. However, I still felt I needed to cover my religion. I was raised Catholic, but currently I do not affiliate with any particular religion. I believe in a higher power and an afterlife, but I claim to be a more spiritual than religious person. When I spoke with interviewees about continuing bonds and re-membering, religious and spiritual topics would often come up. I would tone down any past questioning I ever had about Christianity since leaving my hometown. I felt that the rewards of building relationships with interviewees outweighed the costs of not being able to express my views on some forms of contemporary Christianity.

I found that the spaces of the field heightened my awareness of various covering processes. Through the interactive interviews (Ellis, Kiesinger, & Tillman-Healy, 1997), I found that I had many preconceived notions about what residents of DuQuoin would think about me. Many times, I discovered disappointment about some aspects of my previous self. Doing the interviews and reflecting on my role as a researcher allowed me to see that "reflexivity entails taking seriously the self's location in culture and scholarship, circumspectly exploring our relationship to/in autoethnography, to make research and cultural life *better* and *more meaningful*" (Berry, 2013, p. 212). This life can be better and more meaningful because of autoethnographic reflexivity, even though we may not be happy with certain aspects of our past. My specific methodologies—autoethnography (Ellis & Bochner, 2000; Ellis, 2004) and interactive interviewing (Ellis et al., 1997)—helped me be my best reflexive and researching self—not only during my fieldwork but also in my subsequent interactions with the residents of my hometown.

Autoethnography connects the personal experience of the researcher to cultural phenomena. By engaging in autoethnography, researchers transform their personal experiences into topics of investigation to invite readers to live vicariously through them. For example, Ellis (1993) has written about experiencing the sudden death of her brother in a plane crash, showing readers her own emotions but also the differences in her family members' ways of coping and small-town community rituals for bereavement. Ellis (2004) argues that an autoethnography should evoke in readers a feeling that the experience described is lifelike, believable, and possible.

I have used autoethnography to construct accounts of my continued relationship with my mother (Paxton, 2013; Paxton, 2014; Rennels & Paxton, 2013). When I first started doing autoethnographic research on this topic, it was the first time that I had ever written about my mother's illness and death. In order to create narrative scenes, I had to free-write about my memories of her illness, her death, and our moments together in my childhood. Questions I asked myself when writing included *How did I feel in this moment? What was I thinking? What was said between individuals? What was the setting? What did I see, smell, and touch?* Since the death happened ten years ago, there were times I needed to ask family members questions about the events.

Furthermore, I chose to incorporate my past articles into my process in order to assess how my feelings of grief had changed and what other feelings these works evoked in me, other readers, and our engagement with the texts together. I read all of my autoethnographic articles about my mother and took notes on which parts of the narratives would fit within the larger story of this book. Examples are scenes from observing my mother's illness, the day of her death, and moments of emotionally engaging with artifacts that represented her. While some scenes about my mother's death may look similar to ones in previously published articles, they are not replicas. Rather, they include expanded dialogue and setting descriptions. For example, in chapter 1, I give a fuller description of my time working in the Italian restaurant during high school. I tried to build dramatic tension about my mother's impending death, given that my co-workers were acting differently.

Next, after reading these articles, I created journal entries that explored whether any of my feelings or memories had changed (or whether I remembered new details) about the events of my mother's illness and death. I took notes on how reading scenes of these experiences helped trigger memories for new scenes. For example, I found that many of my feelings during my mother's visitation and funeral were consistent with how I remembered feeling at the time (as depicted in chapter 1). However, I had forgotten that I had felt some resentment toward a few attendees at her visitation. These were people who had been verbally abusive to me. I also had forgotten about a young woman (who I thought I was romantically interested in) attending my mother's visitation. I included this detail to show readers how I struggled with being gay while grieving my mother's death.

Finally, I shared these articles with interviewees during interactive interviews, not only to help me produce a more evocative and vivid account of the events of my mother's illness and death, but also to help guide the conversation during the interviews. I did not remember how my mother and father broke the news to my brother and me about my mother's tumor. Interviewing my father helped fill in the gaps about this event. There were times when I chose to not include a detail I had forgotten about an event—one that an interviewee had remembered. For example, my brother remembered seeing medical staff try to revive my mother with shock treatments. I'm assuming I did not remember this because it was too painful. Even though I chose not to include this detail in the narrative, it did provide some interesting insight into how my brother's coping process was different than mine. Throughout the research process, I had to decide whether to include such forgotten details. I found speaking with interviewees helpful in making these decisions.

Sometimes my past work would come up organically in an interview. Other times, I would ask an interviewee to read one of my articles before an interview. One example in which this proved extremely beneficial was when I asked my stepmother, Kelly, to read my article on transforming minor bodily stigmas through continuing bonds (Paxton, 2013). In this article, I discuss how re-membering my mother helped me cope with my self-consciousness about having excess body hair. This article shared scenes of my mother's illness and death. Kelly had known my mother. However, she was not aware of certain information about my mother's illness and death. Asking her to read the article helped her understand my grief and this research project.

I found that interactive interviewing was needed to enhance relational intimacy with interviewees. Interactive interviewing is an approach used to gain intimate and new understandings of people's experiences with sensitive topics (Ellis et al., 1997). Interactive interviews take place in small group settings and require sufficient time, as well as specific attention to communication and emotions. Because the goal is to gain intimate and new understandings, several interview sessions often are required. It is also ideal that interviewees have a history together or be open to developing strong ties. In addition, both researchers and interviewees should have personal experience with the research topic. All of these requirements coincide with my project, as I interviewed individuals with whom I shared a particular relationship— that of my deceased mother.

I conducted a total of 16 interviews. Some were one-on-one (e.g., an interview with my father, brother, and stepmother), and others were conducted in groups (e.g., my mother's sisters, a couple who were family friends, and a former client mother-daughter pair). Interviews lasted

APPENDIX

between two and three hours. My interviewees were recruited through the use of Facebook messaging, email, and word of mouth from other interviewees. When requesting an interview, I gave a brief written description of the project and requirements for participating. Individuals were given at least two weeks to ask questions and make a decision to participate. Some informal conversations occurred during fieldwork, which were beneficial for the research. Most often these were conversations with family members and friends who I had already formally interviewed for the project. Rather than disrupt mores of personal conversation, I would consult with interviewees after speaking with them. This was to ensure that I could use information they provided me for certain narrative scenes.

For the 16 interactive interviews, I found it best to structure questions similarly to the questions Hedtke (2012) asks individuals in re-membering bereavement support groups. As one of the founding scholars of re-membering processes for the deceased, Hedtke constructed a guidebook for people who wish to construct bereavement support groups that use re-membering rituals and conversations. The bereaved are able to speak about what the deceased "would" say without appearing delusional. Hedtke concludes, "This form of languaging, that of imagined possibility, enables the deceased to become gentle and loving guides" (p. 95). She recommends that facilitators start re-membering conversations in these groups with the question "Can you introduce me to your loved one?" (p. 56). Facilitators are then instructed to ask follow-up questions such as "Who were they? What things did they enjoy in life? What were their professions? What were their hobbies and interests? What kinds of things did you enjoy about them? What did it mean to have them in your life?" (p. 56).

Once the relationship with the deceased has been re-established, Hedtke states that the bereaved may begin to think about other, deeper questions, such as "If your loved one were here, what would he say that he valued about you? What would she say she appreciated about how you were during their illness? What would he say he appreciated about how you have handled things since he died?" (p. 96). Hedtke also recommends that interviewees bring in artifacts of the deceased. I asked my interviewees to do the same, to help facilitate our re-membering conversations. I also reviewed artifacts on my own that I collected from interviewees, including, but not limited to, my mother's obituary, the funeral

155

guest book, and items from private memorials done since the funeral. Sometimes I would bring items of my own to the interviews, to stimulate memories and conversation.

Some of my interview questions were determined ahead of time. However, the interactive interview situations were flexible enough for new questions to emerge. The lines between researcher and interviewee tended to blur in these types of interviews, and these situations empowered interviewees to engage in their own processes of knowledge production. For example, during an interview with my mother's closest friends from her graduating class, many of them discussed several behaviors they had never conceptualized as re-membering. After I completed the project, these women and other interviewees expressed to me rituals they either started doing or recognize routine activities as ways of continuing bonds with the deceased.

Since we were discussing past experiences of loss, I worried that there would be a possibility of re-traumatizing interviewees. However, with every methodological approach one can never predict how interviewees will react to a research study. Doing this type of research allowed me (and required me) to go above and beyond basic IRB protocols to protect my interviewees. Not only did I want to continue bonds with my deceased mother, but also I wanted to continue bonds with those still in my life. I wanted to be the most ethical researcher in the field I could be—given the sensitive nature of the topic.

Ellis (1995) has discussed at length the ethical dilemmas she faced when bringing research back to the interviewees in the Fisher Folk community. Some of these individuals were angry with Ellis and how she represented them—even though she was only attempting to write descriptions of their lives from fieldwork observations. She developed deep friendships with many of these community members and felt pain when she returned to the field after the completion of her book to find many of them were hurt and disappointed with her. Sometimes interviewees will react negatively to your work even when, as a researcher, you believe nothing in your descriptions could be threatening or damaging to their lives. Narrative truth can be tricky, because no matter how much you try to write an experience "as it actually happened," you will never accomplish this feat. And the representations you craft of specific people or events may directly contradict another's perceptions. In the next section, I outline some of these relational quandaries while representing transcript data.

Finding the Narrative Truth of Experience and the Representation of Transcript Data

A traditional colloquialism is "We cannot change our pasts." However, any recounting of a past event can never fully present exactly what happened. As Maxwell (1980) argues:

> What we, or at any rate what I, refer to confidently as memory—meaning a moment, a scene, a fact that has been subjected to a fixative and thereby rescued from oblivion—is really a form of storytelling that goes on continually in the mind and often changes with the telling. Too many conflicting emotional interests are involved for life ever to be wholly acceptable, and possibly it is the work of the storyteller to rearrange things so that they conform to this end. In any case, in talking about the past we lie with every breath we draw.
>
> (p. 27)

This does not mean autoethnographers should not care about the past or how we represent it. Every representation of my own personal experience and the experience of others will never be completely "accurate." However, "it is important to be able to story ourselves, to have a story to tell, and to tell it as well as we can" (Ellis, 2008, p. 15).

In autoethnographic projects, researchers can consult interviewees about how the narrative scenes should be written up (not just descriptions of people or experiences but also whether pseudonyms should be used). Researchers and interviewees do not always agree on every representation, but it is necessary that researchers do all that they can to minimize harm. In rare instances, it may be best not to share certain scenes, to protect a particular relationship or ensure the safety of an interviewee. When researchers are faced with these types of scenarios, they may change particular details of an event or use pseudonyms. This type of literary license is commonly practiced in ethnographic studies. However, the process of adapting interview transcripts into narrative scenes should be done with great care.

In my adaptation process, I transcribed all 16 interviews and chose which ones I thought would best serve as narrative scenes. During this decision making process, I thought about which interviews would not only provide material for the most evocative scenes but also represent the depth and breadth of re-membering practices among members in my mother's community of grievers. In the scene with Sarah depicted in chapter 3, I combined information from three interviews and created a scene with a composite character. I did this because I felt that including too many scenes of individual interviews would slow down the narrative. By creating the composite character of Sarah, I was able to adhere to the essence of how several clients of my mother's re-membered her. In my interview with my mother's sisters, one of the sisters could not attend the scheduled time. I did a one-on-one interview with this sister and adapted her interview into the scene of the group interview.

After writing up narrative scenes, I emailed the drafts to my interviewees and asked for feedback. The reactions varied. Some interviewees were affirming in their responses. One of them stated, "What a great paper! It made me cry all over again! Ann was one in a million!" She then told me about an upcoming family trip to Tampa and asked if I would want to meet her family for dinner. Other interviewees enjoyed their narrative scenes, but they were particular about certain details. For instance, in the scene with my mother's friends from high school (chapter 3), I mistakenly mixed up a few of the interviewees' statements. A couple of her friends informed me of this. I apologized and fixed my mistake.

Interviewees also enjoyed giving feedback on scenes in which they were not depicted. Many stated that after reading parts of my story they remembered things about my mother and her experiences they had forgotten. Some also gained insight into other interviewees' grieving experiences. For example, one of my aunts said she had not realized my father felt so much guilt about my mother's death. The scene in which I visit my grandmother (chapter 3) also greatly touched one of my mother's best friends. "I didn't realize it was still that difficult for Jo-Ann. Reading your work makes me appreciate the time I have with my daughters now," she said. After he read several of my narratives, my brother shared that he felt closer to me. "I knew you were going through a lot when Mom died, but I didn't realize how afraid you were of being rejected," he stated.

As with most autoethnographic projects, I still grapple with some issues of narrative representation. For example, I wondered how the

APPENDIX

narrative scene with my mother's sisters (chapter 3) would impact the relationship between Aunt Cindy and Aunt Patty. After reading the scene, neither of them said anything about the section in which I describe their troubled relationship. I assume they were both aware of their problems. However, during a recent trip home, I heard from my father that he ran into them eating dinner together at a local restaurant. This was surprising, considering the continuing strife between them that we always heard about.

I also considered how this work might impact my relationship with my stepmother. After having her read certain sections and conversing about them, I believe it did not affect our relationship. There was a recent change in holiday family traditions that I believe may have been influenced by the research. Typically, on Christmas Eve and Christmas Day, I attend functions for all three sides of my family (my father's, mother's, and stepmother's). My brother accompanies me, and my father usually only goes to his side and Kelly's side of the family. During this year's Christmas festivities, after visiting with Kelly's family, my father went with my brother and me to see my mother's family. I hope this indicates that reading my work facilitated a better understanding about how to negotiate my father's continued involvement with my mother's family.

After many days of reviewing interview transcripts, I found that the analysis of ethnographic data could be arduous. Not only did I wonder whether I was representing everything in the most ethical way, but I wondered whether I had captured all the information available to me. Might there be a theme that I hadn't found in the data? Was there more an interviewee could have said about a particular experience? Should I interview more people or do more follow-up interviews? These and other questions lingered while I finished this project. However, I realized that, as with the death of a loved one, there would not be a complete resolution. Just as I would continue a relationship with the dead, I would also continue a relationship with this project. Even after the last draft of this book is turned in and published, my analytical work (as well as my mourning process) will never be completely done.

In his comparison of analysis to mourning, Astrachan (2013) argues, "Mourning in this sense is to be understood not as the usual grieving and sorrow following a loss, but—rather paradoxically—as a continuous preserving and safeguarding of the disappearance, absence, and hiddenness of god" (p. 243). I would add this preserving is for the dead as well.

Through several etymological tracings, Astrachan argues that an effective way of conceptualizing the definition of analysis is as an unweaving or a loosening process. Many individuals think of analytic processes as a way to come up with definitive answers to various problems. However, in Astrachan's view, analysis as unweaving can be an "un-working of soul material" (p. 244). Whether we analyze data or dream at night, we create a space to grapple with the uncertainties of our lives—a space to free the soul from the objective psyche. We open a space to loosen the plaguing sorrow brought upon us by a loved one's death. In my case, I was also loosening a tight web of negativity I had spun in my life—about the culture of a space that caused me fear.

Furthermore, Astrachan concludes that when we try to make sense of our lives we continue to return to "nodal points of conflict, to the holes created in the past and to the past where the fabric has become forgotten, knotted, damaged, tangled or torn, where the material lies open and gaping" (p. 252). He continues:

> In the oscillations of the analytic relationship, in the back and forth, we try to piece the material back together, to see where there are fits, joinings, meetings, and meanings. That is, perhaps, the alchemical *opus magnum*, the great work: attempting to create something solid, physical, tangible and material, like gold, like a fabric, a soft purple shawl the color of grapes, or like the philosopher's stone, rough and weighty: and yet also and at the same time, to construct something entirely immaterial, ineffable, and invisible.
>
> (p. 252)

In this project, you see the "great work" of analysis through my exploration of continuing bonds with the living through bonds with the deceased. Holding on to and letting go of the dead are not mutually exclusive processes.

A loved one's death is a rupture in time—a rupture in which, I realize, the work of mourning and analysis is always occurring. As I attempt to understand and let go of sadness, I find that I may reach for these feelings again. I believe I do this in an attempt to feel closer not only to the deceased but also to the individuals who mourn with me. I hold on to these feelings of grief to help me realize that there is more to life than the material reality I experience. Many religious teachings bring up

APPENDIX

the prospect of reuniting with the dead in the afterlife. By having information about continuing bonds, I can go to bed at night confident in the knowledge that I can reunite with the dead in the physical world—whether it's through re-membering, autoethnography, or the process of analysis itself. Perhaps I can go to bed not feeling guilty about my desire to meet the dead in my dreams.

REFERENCES

Adams, T. E. (2006). Seeking father: Reframing a troubled love story. *Qualitative Inquiry*, *12*(4), 704–723. https://doi.org/10.1177/1077800406288607

Astrachan, G. D. (2013). Analysis as mourning. *International Journal of Jungian Studies*, *5*(3), 243–253. http://dx.doi.org/10.1080/19409052.2013.795184

Attig, T. (2001). Relearning the world: Making meaning and finding meanings. In R. Neimeyer (Ed.), *Meaning reconstruction & the experience of loss* (pp. 33–54). Washington, DC: American Psychological Association.

Baxter, L. A., & Braithwaite, D. O. (2006). Family rituals. In L. H. Turner & R. West (Eds.), *The family communication sourcebook* (pp. 259–280). Thousand Oaks, CA: Sage.

Becker, E. (1973). *The denial of death*. New York, NY: Macmillan Publishing.

Becvar, D. S. (2001). *In the presence of grief*. New York, NY: Guilford Press.

Behar, R. (1996). *The vulnerable observer: Anthropology that breaks your heart*. Boston, MA: Beacon.

Bennett, G., & Bennett, K. M. (2000). The presence of the dead: An empirical study. *Mortality*, *5*(2), 139–157.

Bennett, M. K. (2010). "You can't spend years with someone and just cast them aside": Augmented identity in older British widows. *Journal of Women & Aging*, *22*(3), 204–217. http://dx.doi.org/10.1080/08952841.2010.495571

Berns, N. (2011). *Closure: The rush to end grief and what it costs us*. Philadelphia, PA: Temple University Press.

Berry, K. (2013). Spinning autoethnographic reflexivity, cultural critique, and negotiating selves. In S. H. Jones, T. E. Adams, & C. Ellis (Eds.), *Handbook of autoethnography* (pp. 209–227). Walnut Creek, CA: Left Coast Press.

Berzoff, J. (2011). The transformative nature of grief and bereavement. *Clinical Social Work Journal*, *39*(3), 262–269. doi: 10.1007/s10615-011-0317-6

Biank, N. M., & Werner-Lin, A. (2011). Growing up with grief: Revisiting the death of a parent over the life course. *Omega*, *63*, 271–290. https://doi.org/10.2190/OM.63.3.e

Bochner, A. P. (1997). It's about time: Narrative and the divided self. *Qualitative Inquiry, 3*(4), 418–438. https://doi.org/10.1177/107780049700300404

Bochner, A. P. (2009). "Communication's calling: The importance of what we care about." Presidential address, National Communication Association, November 23, 2008, Chicago. *Spectra, 45*(January), 14–29.

Bowlby, J. (1961). Processes of mourning. *International Journal of Psychoanalysis, 42*, 317–340. doi: 13872076

Boyd, D. M., & Ellison, N. B. (2008). Social network sites: Definition, history, and scholarship. *Journal of Computer-Mediated Communication, 13*, 210–230. doi: 10.1111/j.1083-6101.2007.00393.x

Boylorn, R. M. (2009). *Southern black women: Their lived realities* (unpublished doctoral dissertation). University of South Florida, Tampa, FL.

Boylorn, R. M. (2012). *Sweetwater: Black women and narratives of resilience.* New York, NY: Peter Lang Publishing.

Braithwaite, D. O., Bach, B. W., Baxter, L. A., DiVerniero, R., Hammonds, J. R., Hosek, A. M., . . . Wolf, B. M. (2010). Constructing family: A typology of voluntary kin. *Journal of Personal Relationships, 27*(3), 388–407. https://doi.org/10.1177/0265407510361615

Brent, D., Melhem, N., Donohoe, B., & Walker, M. (2009). The incidence and course of depression in bereaved youth 21 months after the loss of a parent to suicide, accident, or sudden natural death. *American Journal of Psychiatry, 166*(7), 786–794. https://doi.org/10.1176/appi.ajp.2009.08081244

Brison, S. J. (1997). Outliving oneself: Trauma, memory, and personal identity. In D. T. Meyers (Ed.), *Feminists rethink the self* (pp. 12–39). Boulder, CO: Westview Press.

Bruner, J. (1987). Life as narrative. *Social Research, 54*, 11–32. Retrieved from www.jstor.org/stable/40970444

Cacciatore, J., & Flint, M. (2012). Mediating grief: Postmortem ritualization after child death. *Journal of Loss & Trauma, 17*, 158–172. http://dx.doi.org/10.1080/15325024.2011.595299

Cameron, J. (Producer), & Cameron, J. (Director). (1997). *Titanic* (Motion picture). United States: Paramount Pictures.

Carr, D., House, J., Wortman, C., Nesse, R., & Kessler, R. (2001). Psychological adjustment to sudden and anticipated spousal loss among older widowed persons. *The Journals of Gerontology Series B: Psychological Sciences and Social Sciences, 56*, S237–S248. https://doi.org/10.1093/geronb/56.4.S237

Chatters, L. M., Taylor, R. J., & Jayakody, R. (1994). Fictive kinship relations in black extended families. *Journal of Comparative Family Studies, 25*, 297–313. Retrieved from www.jstor.org/stable/41602341

Clark, K. B. (1989). *Dark ghetto: Dilemmas of social power.* Indianapolis, IN: Wesleyan Publishing.

Clements, P. T., DeRanieri, J. T., & Benasutti, K. M. (2004). Life after death: Grief therapy after the sudden and traumatic death of a family member. *Perspectives in Psychiatric Care, 40*, 149–154. doi: 10.1111/j.1744-6163.2004.tb00012.x

Corr, C. A., & Corr, D. M. (2013). *Death and dying, life and living* (7th ed.). Belmont, CA: Wadsworth, Cengage Learning.

References

Davis, C. S. (2010). *Death: The beginning of a relationship*. Cresskill, NJ: Hampton Press.

DeGroot, J. M. (2012). Maintaining relational continuity with the deceased on Facebook. *Omega, 65*(3), 195–212. https://doi.org/10.2190/OM.65.3.c

Ellis, C. (1991). Sociological introspection and emotional experience. *Symbolic Interaction, 14*(1), 23–50. doi: 10.1525/si.1991.14.1.23

Ellis, C. (1993). There are survivors: Telling a story of sudden death. *Sociological Quarterly, 34*(4), 711–730. Retrieved from www.jstor.org/stable/4121376

Ellis, C. (1995). Emotional and ethical quagmires in returning to the field. *Journal of Contemporary Ethnography, 24*(1), 68–98. https://doi.org/10.1177/089124195024001003

Ellis, C. (2003). Grave tending with mom at the cemetery. *Forum Qualitative Sozialforschung/Forum: Qualitative Social Research, 4*(2), Art. 28. Retrieved from http://nbn-resolving.de/urn:nbn:de:0114-fqs0302285

Ellis, C. (2004). *The ethnographic I: A methodological novel about autoethnography*. Walnut Creek, CA: AltaMira Press.

Ellis, C. (2008). *Revision: Autoethnographic reflections on life and work*. Walnut Creek, CA: Left Coast Press.

Ellis, C. (2013). Seeking my brother's voice: Holding onto long-term grief through photographs, stories, and reflections. In E. Miller (Ed.), *Stories of complicated grief: A critical anthology* (pp. 1–31). Washington, DC: NASW (National Association of Social Workers Press).

Ellis, C., & Bochner, A. P. (1992). Telling and performing personal stories: The constraints of choice in abortion. In C. Ellis & M. J. Flaherty (Eds.), *Investigating subjectivity: Research on lived experience* (pp. 79–101). Newbury Park, CA: Sage Publications.

Ellis, C., & Bochner, A. P. (2000). Autoethnography, personal narrative, reflexivity. In N. K. Denzin & Y. S. Lincoln (Eds.), *Handbook of qualitative research* (pp. 733–768). Thousand Oaks, CA: Sage.

Ellis, C., Kiesinger, C. E., & Tillman-Healy, L. (1997). Interactive interviewing: Talking about emotional experience. In R. Hertz (Ed.), *Reflexivity and voice* (pp. 119–149). Thousand Oaks, CA: Sage.

Fletcher, D. (2009, October 28). What happens to your Facebook after you die? *Time Magazine Online*. Retrieved from http://content.time.com/time/business/article/0,8599,1932803,00.html

Foster, T. L., Gilmer, M. J., Davies, B., Dietrich, M. S., Barrera, M., Fairclough, D. L., Vannatta, K., & Gerhardt, C. A. (2011). Comparison of continuing bonds reported by parents and siblings after a child's death from cancer. *Death Studies, 35*(5), 420–440. http://dx.doi.org/10.1080/07481187.2011.553308

Frank, A. (1991). *At the will of the body: Reflections on illness*. Boston, MA: Houghton Mifflin.

Frank, A. (1995). *The wounded storyteller: Body, illness, and ethics*. Chicago, IL: Chicago University Press.

Freeman, M. (2010). *Hindsight: The promise and peril of looking backward*. New York, NY: Oxford University Press.

References

Freud, S. (1961). Mourning and melancholia. In J. Strachey (Ed. and Trans.), *The standard edition of the complete psychological works of Sigmund Freud* (Vol. 14, pp. 243–258). London, England: Hogwarth Press. (Original work published 1917)

Gamino, L. A., Sewell, K. W., & Easterling, L. W. (1998). Scott and White Grief Study: An empirical test of predictors of intensified mourning. *Death Studies, 26,* 793–813. http://dx.doi.org/10.1080/074811898201524

Geertz, C. (1973). *The interpretation of cultures.* New York, NY: Harper Collins.

Hedtke, L. (2012). *Bereavement support groups: Breathing life into the stories of the dead.* Chagrin Falls, OH: Taos Institute Publications.

Hedtke, L., & Winslade, J. (2004). *Remembering lives: Conversations with the dying and the bereaved.* Amityville, NY: Baywood Publishing Co.

Hegedus, K., Zana, A., & Szabo, G. (2008). Effect of end of life education on medical students' and health care workers' death attitude. *Palliative Medicine, 22*(3), 264–269. https://doi.org/10.1177/0269216307086520

Hieftje, K. (2012). The role of social networking sites in memorialization of college students. In C. J. Sofka, I. Noppe Cupit, & K. R. Gilbert (Eds.), *Dying, death, and grief in an online universe: For counselors and educators.* New York, NY: Springer Publishing Company.

Hochschild, A. R. (1983). *The managed heart: Commercialization of human feeling.* Los Angeles, CA: University of California Press.

Ibsen, C. A., & Klobus, P. (1972). Fictive kin term use in social relationships: Alternative interpretations. *Journal of Marriage and the Family, 34,* 615–620. Retrieved from www.jstor.org/stable/350312

Jorgenson, J., & Bochner, A. P. (2004). Imagining families through stories and rituals. In A. L. Vangelisti (Ed.), *Handbook of family communication* (pp. 513–538). Mahwah, NJ: Lawrence Erlbaum.

Kalish, R. A. (1981). *Death, grief, and caring relationships.* Pacific Grove, CA: Brooks/ Cole Publishing.

Kalish, R. A., & Reynolds, D. K. (1976). *Death and ethnicity: A psychocultural study.* Los Angeles, CA: University of Southern California Press.

Keeley, M. P. (2004). Final conversations: Survivors' memorable messages concerning religious faith and spirituality. *Health Communication, 16*(1), 87–104. http://dx.doi.org/10.1207/S15327027HC1601_6

Kellehear, A. (1984). Are we a death denying society? A sociological review. *Social Science and Medicine, 18*(9), 713–723. https://doi.org/10.1016/0277-9536(84)90094-7

Kempson, D., & Murdock, V. (2010). Memory keepers: A narrative study on siblings never known. *Death Studies, 34*(8), 738–756. http://dx.doi.org/10.1080/07481181003765402

Klass, D. (1993). Solace and immortality: Bereaved parents' continuing bond with their children. *Death Studies, 17,* 343–368. http://dx.doi.org/10.1080/07481189308252630

Klass, D. (1997). The deceased child in the psychic and social worlds of bereaved parents during the resolution of grief. *Death Studies, 21,* 147–175. http://dx.doi.org/10.1080/074811897202056

References

Klass, D. (2006). Continuing conversations about continuing bonds. *Death Studies*, *30*, 843–858. http://dx.doi.org/10.1080/07481180600886959

Klass, D., Silverman, D., & Nickman, S. (1996). *Continuing bonds: New understandings of grief*. Washington, DC: Taylor & Francis.

Klugman, C. M. (2006). Dead men talking: Evidence of post-death contact and continuing bonds. *Omega—Journal of Death and Dying, 53*, 249–262. https://doi.org/10.2190/40UP-PKC5-D4RV-E1QV

Koenig Kellas, J., & Trees, A. R. (2006). Finding meaning in difficult family experiences: Sense-making and interaction processes during joint family storytelling. *Journal of Family Communication, 6*(1), 49–76. http://dx.doi.org/10.1207/s15327698jfc0601_4

Kubler-Ross, E. (1969). *On death and dying*. New York, NY: Routledge.

Kuhn, T. (1962). *The structure of scientific revolutions*. Chicago, IL: Chicago University Press.

Langellier, K. M., & Peterson, E. E. (2006). Family storytelling as communication practice. In L. H. Turner & R. West (Eds.), *The family communication sourcebook* (pp. 119–124). Thousand Oaks, CA: Sage.

LeRoy, M. (Producer), & Fleming, V. (Director). (1939). *The Wizard of Oz* (Motion picture). United States: MGM Studios.

Marwick, A., & Ellison, N. B. (2012). "There isn't wifi in heaven!" Negotiating visibility on Facebook memorial pages. *Journal of Broadcasting and Electronic Media, 56*(3), 378–400. http://dx.doi.org/10.1080/08838151.2012.705197

Marwit, S. J., & Klass, D. (1996). Grief and the role of inner representation of the deceased. In D. Klass, P. R. Silverman, & S. L. Nickman (Eds.), *Continuing bonds: New understandings of grief* (pp. 297–308). Washington, DC: Taylor & Francis.

Maxwell, W. (1980). *So long, see you tomorrow*. New York, NY: Knopf.

Muraco, A. (2006). Intentional families: Fictive kin ties between cross gender, different sexual orientation friends. *Journal of Marriage & Family, 68*, 1313–1325. doi: 10.1111/j.1741-3737.2006.00330.x

Neimeyer, R. A. (2001). The language of loss: Grief therapy as a process of meaning reconstruction. In R. Neimeyer (Ed.), *Meaning reconstruction & the experience of loss* (pp. 261–292). Washington, DC: American Psychological Association.

Packman, W., Horsley, H., Davies, B., & Kramer, R. (2006). Sibling bereavement and continuing bonds. *Death Studies, 30*, 817–841. http://dx.doi.org/10.1080/07481180600886603

Parkes, C. M. (1975). Determinants of outcome following bereavement. *Omega—Journal of Death and Dying, 6*, 303–323. https://doi.org/10.2190/PR0R-GLPD-5FPB-422L

Parkes, C. M., & Prigerson, H. (2010). *Bereavement: Studies of grief in adult life* (4th ed.). New York, NY: Routledge.

Paxton, B. A. (2013). Transforming minor bodily stigmas through holding onto grief: A "hair raising" possibility. *Qualitative Inquiry, 19*(5), 355–365. https://doi.org/10.1177/1077800413479561

Paxton, B. A. (2014). Queerly conversing with the dead: Re-membering mom. *Cultural Studies - Critical Methodologies, 14*(2), 164–173. https://doi.org/10.1177/1532708613512273

References

Paxton, B. A. (2017). Speaking to and theorizing about the dead in a postmodern world: An autoethnographic possibility? *Qualitative Research Journal, 17*(1), 20–31. https://doi.org/10.1108/QRJ-01-2016-0005

Peters, J. D. (2001). *Speaking into the air: A history of the idea of communication.* Chicago, IL: University of Chicago Press.

Rennels, T. R., & Paxton, B. A. (2013). Sudden death, sudden friend: Exploring the role of friendship and continuing bonds with the deceased. *Qualitative Communication Research, 2*(2), 182–212. doi: 10.1525/qcr.2013.2.2.182

Root, B. L., & Exline, J. J. (2014). The role of continuing bonds in coping with grief: Overview and future directions. *Death Studies, 38*, 1–8. http://dx.doi.org/10.1080/07481187.2012.712608

Rostila, M., & Saarela, J. M. (2011). Time does not heal all wounds: Mortality following the death of a parent. *Journal of Marriage and Family, 73*, 236–249. doi: 10.1111/j.1741-3737.2010.00801.x

Russac, R. J., Steighner, N. S., & Canto, A. I. (2002). Grief work versus continuing bonds: A call for paradigm integration or replacement? *Death Studies, 26*, 463–478. http://dx.doi.org/10.1080/074811802760138996

Schenck, D. P., & Roscoe, L. A. (2009). In search of a good death. *Journal of Medical Humanities, 30*(1), 61–72. https://doi.org/10.1007/s10912-008-9071-3

Seale, C. (1998). *Constructing death.* Cambridge, MA: Cambridge University Press.

Sofka, C. J., Noppe Cupit, I., & Gilbert, K. R. (2012). Thanatechnology as a conduit for living, dying, and grieving in contemporary society. In C. J. Sofka, I. Noppe Cupit, & K. R. Gilbert (Eds.), *Dying, death, and grief in an online universe: For counselors and educators* (pp. 3–15). New York: Springer.

Sprengnether, M. (2002). Surrender: Shadowlands. In M. Sprengnether, *Crying at the movies: A film memoir* (pp. 154–180). Minneapolis, MN: Graywolf Press.

Stroebe, M. S., Abakoumkin, G., Stroebe, W., & Schut, H. (2011). Continuing bonds in adjustment to bereavement: Impact of abrupt versus gradual separation. *Personal Relationships, 1111*(10), 1–12. doi: 10.1111/j.1475-6811.2011.01352.x

Tucker, T. (2009). Culture of death denial: Relevant or rhetoric in medical education? *Journal of Palliative Medicine, 12*(12), 1105–1108. https://doi.org/10.1089/jpm.2009.0234

Tyson-Rawson, K. (1996). Relationship and heritage: Manifestations of ongoing attachment following father death. In D. Klass, D. Silverman, & S. Nickman (Eds.), *Continuing bonds: New understandings of grief* (pp. 125–145). London, England: Taylor & Francis.

Valentine, C. (2008). *Bereavement narratives: Continuing bonds in the twenty-first century.* New York, NY: Routledge.

Vanzant, I. (2012). *Peace from broken pieces: How to get through what you are going through.* New York, NY: SmileyBooks.

Walter, T., Hourizi, R., Moncur, W., & Pitsillides, S. (2011). Does the internet change how we die and mourn? Overview and analysis. *Omega—Journal of Death and Dying, 64*(4), 275–302. https://doi.org/10.2190/OM.64.4.a

References

Williams, A. L., & Merten, M. J. (2009). Adolescents' online social networking following the death of a peer. *Journal of Adolescent Research, 24*(1), 67–90. https://doi.org/10.1177/0743558408328440

Worden, J. W. (1991). *Grief counseling and grief therapy: A handbook for the mental health practitioner*. New York, NY: Springer Publishing Company.

Yoshino, K. (2007). *Covering: The hidden assault on our civil rights*. New York, NY: Random House.

Zimmerman, C., & Rodin, G. (2004). The denial of death thesis: Sociological critique and implications for palliative care. *Palliative Medicine, 18*(2), 121–128. https://doi.org/10.1191/0269216304pm858oa

INDEX

Adams, T. E. 140
analysis 159–160
anger 129
Astrachan, G. D. 159–160
Attig, T. 112
autoethnography: and common experiences 52–53, 152; and continuing relationships 7, 152–154; and cultural phenomena 152; and interviewing 151–157; methodology 149–160; narratives of 156–157; and storytelling 149–150

Bach, B. W. 138
Baxter, L. A. 113, 138
Becker, E. 122
bereavement: and communities 6–7; and continuing bonds 3–4, 7; culture of 149; and guilt 128–129; process of 3, 6, 150; and reflection 111–112; and re-membering rituals 111–115, 121–122, 143; support for 5; *see also* grief
bereavement support groups 155
Berns, N. 127
Berry, K. 149
Bochner, A. P. 142
Braithwaite, D. O. 113, 138

causality thesis 110–111
chaos narratives 121

children's death 124
closure 7, 112, 127
communication: post-death 62, 115; as social construction 54; and technology 132–133
communities 6–7
continuing bonds: analysis of 160; and bereaved individuals 3, 6–7, 111–113; causality thesis in 110–111; collective nature of 6; as a coping strategy 8; and distance 124–126; and family relationships 140–141; and grief 5, 126–127; interactions of 110; and loss 141; and post-death contact 112, 139–140; and reflection 111–112; and re-membering rituals 80–81, 111–113; research in 131; role of social media in 131–138; strategies for 4; and voluntary kin 139–140
culture: death-denying 122, 126; and grief 6; webs of 149, 151

Day of the Dead 5
death: and closure 7, 112, 127; and continuing relationships 54; denial of 121–122; and re-membering rituals 121–122
deceased: connection with 3–8, 79–80, 155; re-membering 4, 80–81; signs from 83–85, 112
DeGroot, J. M. 133

dis-membering 113
DiVerniero, R. 138
DuQuoin, Illinois: culture of 14–15;
 memories of 85–87; visiting 66–67

Ellis, C. 7–8, 52–54, 112, 139–140, 152, 155
Ellison, N. B. 133
emotions: anger 129; culturally
 opposed 8; and grief 127–130; guilt
 128–129
Exline, J. J. 6, 131

Facebook memorials 131–138
families: and dis-membering 113;
 narratives of 142; and post-death
 contact 112, 115–117; relationships
 with 140–141; and re-membering
 rituals 111–114; and sense-making
 114–115; and spirituality/religion
 113–114; and stigmatization
 112–113; and storytelling 112,
 114–115; voluntary kin as 138–139
fictive kin 138
Frank, A. 121
Freud, Sigmund 3

Gilbert, K. R. 132
grave visits 112
grief: alternative discourses for 5; and
 analysis 159–160; and closure 127;
 and communities 8; cultural feeling
 rules for 128–129; and culture 6;
 experiences of 7–8; Freud on 3;
 long-term 53–54; perspectives on
 4–5; traditional models of 3, 6–7;
 see also bereavement
guilt 128–129

Hammonds, J. R. 138
Hedtke, L. 4, 111, 113, 121–122, 124, 155
Hieftje, K. 132
Hosek, A. M. 138
Hourizi, R. 132

illness: narratives of 121; see also
 terminal illness
interactive interviewing 152–156
Internet: and loss 132; and
 memorialization 132–138

interviews: emotions during 127–130;
 ethical dilemmas in 155–156,
 159; of friends and family 75–80,
 88–96, 98–109, 116–121, 123–130;
 interactive 152–156; as involved
 observer 151–152; writing narratives
 from 156–159

journal entries 153

Keeley, M. P. 113–114
Kelly, Max 132
Klass, D. 3, 6, 110–111
Koenig Kellas, J. 114

long-term grief 53–54

Marwick, A. 133
Maxwell, W. 156
memorialization: grave visits 112;
 and re-membering rituals 111–113;
 through Facebook 131–138; through
 storytelling 112
Merten, M. J. 133
meta-autoethnography 7
Moncur, W. 132
mothers: loss of 51–52, 54; see also
 Paxton, Ann Elizabeth
"moving on" 112

narratives: chaos 121; quest 121;
 representing 156–159; restitution
 121; of terminal illness 37, 121
Neimeyer, R. A. 4
Nickman, S. 3
Noppe Cupit, I. 132

Paxton, Ann Elizabeth: death of 28–35,
 96–97, 104–105; illness of 17–28,
 94–95, 120–121; re-membering 80,
 87–92, 95, 98–109, 115–121, 134–138;
 salon work 15–17, 118, 136–137
Paxton, Blake: college years 41–48;
 coming out 44–45, 101; and family
 65–72, 81–84, 87–92, 145–148; and
 father 103–109, 140; and grief 66,
 68, 71, 74–75; hometown of 14–15,
 66–67, 85–87; and identity 151–152;
 as involved observer 151–152; and

INDEX

Mark 12–13; and mother's death 29–39, 50–53, 67–68, 70–71, 74; and mother's illness 17–28; and mother's work 15–17; and psychic reading 55–64; relationship with mother 9–12, 15, 19–20, 40–41, 49, 54–55, 63–64, 72–73, 148, 152–153
Paxton, Kyle 16, 18–19, 45–46, 81–82
Peters, J. D. 115
Pitsillides, S. 132
post-death contact 112, 115–117, 139–140
psychic readings 55–64

quest narratives 121

reflection 111–112
religion 113–114
re-membering 4, 54, 110, 142–143
re-membering rituals: and death 121–122; and distance 125–126; at family wedding 147; and friendships 80–81; grave visits 112; memorialization 111–112; and post-death contact 112, 115–117; practices of 115–121, 124; and professions 117–118; and reflection 111–112; and sense-making 114–115; spirituality and religion in 113–114, 151–152; and stigmatization 112–113; and storytelling 111–112, 114–115
restitution narratives 121
Root, B. L. 6, 131

sadness 7–8, 160
sense-making 114–115
Silverman, D. 3
social networking sites (SNSs): and continuing relationships 131–133; and memorialization 132–135, 137–138; re-membering rituals on 135–136
Sofka, C. J. 132
spirituality 113–114
Sprengnether, M. 8
stigmatization 112–113
storytelling 111–112, 114–115, 149–150

terminal illness: and death denial 122; and family storytelling 114; narratives of 37, 121; palliative care for 121; and post-death contact 113
thanatechnology 132
Trees, A. R. 114

Vanzant, Iyanla 65
voluntary kin 138–140

Walter, T. 132
Williams, A. L. 133
Winslade, J. 4, 111, 113, 121–122, 124
Wolf, B. M. 138

Yoshino, K. 151